7 SHADES OF LOVE

An anthology of poems exploring love, loss, joy and forgiveness

Daniella Blechner

7 Shades of Love: Daniella Blechner.

Poetry anthology

Printed in the United Kingdom

First Printing 2014. Conscious Dreams Publishing.
www.consciousdreamspublishing.com

Edited by Daniella Blechner and E Lee Caleca

Images c/o dreamstime

Cover design by Vikncharlie

ISBN: 978-1-915522-41-2

I sincerely thank everyone who contributed their wonderful poems to the '7 Shades of Love' anthology and to everyone who has supported me in cash and in kind, and most importantly, to my Creator who provided me with the lessons, confidence and words to inspire others. Thank you for my lessons in Love- I will never stop learning!

About the Author

Daniella Blechner, author of 'Mr Wrong', is a South London based writer whose real writing journey began writing and directing comedy sketches for Youth Project's 'Phenomenon '98' featuring Gina Yashere and Richard Blackwood.

At 18 years old, she began her career as a performance poet and enjoyed success in bars and clubs in and around London for many years. In 2002, she attended Ravensbourne College where she wrote, produced and directed her first short 'Connexions', which was Nominated for Best Screenplay at the BFM Short Film Awards in 2006 and won Best Open Deck Film when screened at the Cutting East Festival.

Daniella won the 2007 Film Fund Award from Lewisham Film Initiative to complete her poetry-based short drama 'Hair We Are' for the Black History Month Short Film Challenge. 'Hair We Are' won the 3rd Best Film at the Images of Black Women Film Festival and has been screened at Chicago International Children's Film, the Pan African Film Festival in LA, and BAMKids Film Festival in New York. It was also screened on The Community Channel and can be viewed at www.itvlocal.com. Since writing and directing the film, the poem has been included in Shangwe's 'Hair Power, Skin Revolution' anthology founded by Nicole Moore. From here, she has performed her poem at literary events.

She enjoys examining and reflecting on social issues often laced with a wicked sense of humour. She especially enjoys working with young people and those at risk of exclusion from society.

CONTENTS

INTRODUCTION

'What is Love?' I asked my class of twenty pre-pubescent teenage boys. 'Loving an imperfect person perfectly,' declared 14 year old Nikesh from South London. *Loving an imperfect person perfectly*. I stopped dead in my tracks as I pondered this whilst writing on the board. Little did he know that this declaration was to change my life completely.

Whilst I had had many boyfriends who were far from perfect, I had always loved them despite these imperfections. This Love was unconditional. As I wrote these words upon the board, I was a young teacher who'd just been dumped by a man I thought was my knight in shining armour. Unbeknown to me, two years later, I would indeed find out that he was actually engaged with a child the entire ten months of our relationship. I had bags under my eyes from lack of sleep and lesson planning, and I was riddled with insecurity and regret. Did I push him away? Was this my fault? As I wrote these words on the board, I realised that I was my own worst enemy. I battered myself, criticised myself and believed myself to be unworthy. It was I who did not Love *myself* perfectly. It was I who did not realise what I truly deserved.

It was then I realised that there are many types of Love and that Love does not always have to be an outward projection but something that exists and must be exercised internally. For if we do not Love ourselves then how can we expect others to?

'7 Shades of Love' explores the many different ways that we express Love. On a human level, sometimes we may feel that Love means that we need to control another, create a type of co-dependent style of relationship with another and, sometimes even abandon our own selves in honour of another.

7 Shades of Love' concludes that, as Bob Marley said, there is only One Love and that Love is unconditional, non-judgemental and all accepting; loving an imperfect person perfectly!

'7 Shades of Love' explores Love through colours and their associated meanings through both Eastern and Western traditions and beliefs. Poems have been penned from women and men from England, Jamaica, USA, Malaysia, Canada and Kenya, and I hope I have reflected a wealth of beliefs and attitudes towards the Universal theme that connects us: LOVE.

CHAKRAS EXPLAINED

This book delves into the meanings and connotations of all seven colours of the rainbow. To explore this, I have used both Western and Eastern beliefs. One of these beliefs is the body's chakra system.

In Hindu and Buddhist belief systems, it is believed that the body contains seven major energy centres that lie vertically from the tailbone to the crown of our head. Each of these chakras contains energy relating to specific emotional and spiritual needs. Chakra means "wheel" in Sanskrit as it is believed that each chakra rotates in a circular motion like a wheel. Each of these chakras vibrates at a different frequency and sequentially radiates each colour of the rainbow from red to violet.

The chakras act much like vacuums that literally pull mental and emotional energy into the energy centre. It is important to keep this energy fluid and unblocked so that the chakras work in unison creating and keeping us emotionally, mentally and spiritually balanced.

Chakras can be kept clear through meditation and affirmation, and by surrounding yourself with people and environments that are positive and serve your highest good, but most of all, through forgiveness and letting go of negative and harmful belief systems.

The Root Chakra

(Muladhara)

The root chakra is originally known as the *Muladhara* in Sanskrit which means 'root' or 'base'. This is the first energy centre located at the base of our spine or perineum. It rules the lowest vibration in our bodies and vibrates at the slowest wavelength. It is linked to survival, security, and a sense of safety and belonging. According to Maslow's Law[1], survival, safety and a sense of belonging are the greatest basic human needs and help us form a clear picture of who we are in the wider world.

The root chakra grounds us to the Earth and keeps us attached to 'earthly' things and the material world. When this centre is clear we feel secure, grounded and 'earthed'. When it is blocked we feel fearful and insecure; all the pleasure we gain from material goods may become

---

[1] Maslow (1943) created a motivation theory (*hierarchy of needs*) which suggests five Interdependent levels of basic human needs (motivators) that must be satisfied In a strict sequence starting with the lowest level. (See page 91 for more Information)

threatened. We may feel that we do not belong and we may overcompensate through the satisfaction of material things.

When this chakra is overactive we may feel inclined to become angry or aggressive when our ‘fixed ideas’ are challenged. Interestingly, the root chakra is linked to the sense of smell.

Our sense of smell is our most primitive sense and is awakened at birth. The root chakra represents the first two years of life.

Red

Red is a positive and bold colour full of vitality and vigour. It is the colour of blood and fire and so is associated with danger, war, strength, power, and death as well as love, lust, sex, eroticism and passion. It is also linked with determination (blood, sweat and tears) and success. In heraldry it is a colour of courage, strength and valour and is often used in flags and shields.

It is an emotionally charged colour full of intensity and boldness. It excites the viewer and raises blood pressure. Its eye-catching nature forces its viewer to stop, look and listen. It is a colour frequently used for emergency signs, adverts and stop lights to draw attention to its message. Red is the colour for danger and warnings. Red flags go up when we sense danger in our lives.

The bright vitality and bold nature of red is said to stimulate the appetite and enliven our yearnings. It is a colour of desire, lust and sexuality (the Lady in Red, the Scarlet Lady). It can stir and stimulate deeper and more intimate passions within us such as those associated with love and sex.

Too much red, however can irritate the senses and cause aggression and anger.

- ♥ **Dark red:** denotes strength, courage, power, leadership, anger, wrath and revenge
- ♥ **Pink:** the colour of unconditional love, romance and femininity

- **Reddish Brown:** the colour of harvest, Autumn and transformation
- **Brown:** masculine; represents stability and a sense of grounding

'*The true color of life is the color of the body, the color of the covered red, the implicit and not explicit red of the living heart and the pulses. It is the modest color of the unpublished blood.*'

— Alice Meynell[2]

[2] **Alice Christiana Gertrude Meynell** (née Thompson; 22 September 1847 – 27 November 1922) was an English writer, editor, critic, and suffragist, now remembered mainly as a poet.

RED FLAGS

She salivated when she met him
Turned dizzy with adrenaline
Craved him so instantly she let him in
She simply said, 'hello' with a great big grin

He was the kind of man who turned heads
Turned up the heating inside
She was a woman who usually carefully treads
But with him time she did not bide

They say, 'Go slowly and go well.'
She said, 'Go to hell'
'This man is on fire!' but they said, 'Only time will tell.'
She had a thirst that nothing could quell

He was known as a player
But she would change that
So she ignored the naysayers
She was not a doormat

He was different with her- she could see
And who were they to tell her who she should be
'You're just jealous 'cos he's with me.'
'Let me live, let me be free!

He took her to all kinds of places
He made her head spin
Her heart would run races
She felt worthy when she was with him

Her King made her feel safe, loved and desired

To her this was Love- that's all she required
Being with him never grew tired
She was his Queen who he loved and admired

'Be careful,' they said when he pulled out a ring
She wept and screamed 'yes!'
They were only four months in

She moved in at once
She couldn't wait to get started
It was a couple of months
When he frequently departed

He would leave her alone for days on end
When she tried to get hold of him he'd not reply to the texts she'd send
Her security was crushed when he told her my fears were 'pretend.'
Insecurity set in and her self-esteem she could not mend

When she asked him for clarity, he'd see 'red' and point the finger at her
The King was now a man on fire with anger
And she was the coal

Found girls' numbers in his pockets
The scent of perfume on his shirt collar
He laughed and pacified her with gold lockets
Inside she wanted to holler

She would protest and question him
But he would overpower her with the strength of his lies
Her Spirit was crushed- to believe him was just a way to survive

She saw the red flags from the beginning but kept her eyes closed shut
She wanted to believe his pretty lies and honest eyes
His silky words and meaningful 'goodbyes.'
She kept her eyes shut but inside she knew the truth

She was just a pawn in his game
One of many....

Her whole world crushed down; her safety net broke
To him she was a means to an end, to the outside world, a big joke
The embarrassment kills her
She declared to never trust again
10 years on and has lost her faith in all men

'Only time will tell,' they said
To this day these words ring in her head
From when she wakes up to when she sets her head down for bed

She **will** Love again
Love even stronger
When her faith is restored she'll wait that bit longer

She **will** love again
But she'll Love Her Self first
She'll be more discerning and be not blinded by the material
She'll take time to Know the Spirit and appreciate what's Real

Daniella Blechner, 34, London, England
(written 27/12/2013)

THE FEAR INSIDE

I fear what could happen
I fear I could fall
I fear you leaving me
Because I know we could have it all

I'm scared you won't care the same way I do
I'm scared that I could fall in love with you
I'm scared that you'll hurt and break me in ways I've dealt with before
Mostly because my heart really likes you
With each day that passes, more and more

I keep thinking the things you say and do aren't real
Motivated by hidden thoughts
Afraid once you get what you're looking for
Like the rest, you'll go running off
In my heart of hearts, I want to believe in what you say you feel
But I still can't help but wonder if you'll always be here

Athziri, 21 Illinois, USA

RISKY BUSINESS

I'm taking a risk
I'm letting you in
Giving my love
Knowing my heart
Could be broken again

I'm scared as hell
Don't know if it's right
But I'm ready to dive in
And put up the fight

Things could go wrong,
But they could be better than I think
I can't keep living in fear
Scared that you're going to hurt me

I want us to last
To make it through it all
My heart really likes you
And I hope you catch me if I fall

Don't want more disappointment
Another good bye
Another person to tell me or let me know
Everything he said he felt was only a lie

I want that happiness
That love felt by two
The kind that gives me butterflies
Whenever I think of you

Athziri, 21 Illinois, USA

MY GARDEN

In the stillness of the morning
That quiet time of day
Is when I most want your presence
In a very special way
Visit my garden
Smell the fragrance of my flower
Take your time
Make it your home for at least the next hour
Touch the soft petals
Feel the coolness on your hands
Explore the wonders of nature
Watch how the flower blooms on command
Enjoy each precious moment
Until you come again
To visit my garden
Especially after it rains.

Simone Dunbar, Kingston, Jamaica

THE REFUGE OF LOVE - TO MY WIFE

The perfect moment
is the one that I spend
with you. Your touch
keeps still the moving
illusions of time.
I can hear the quiet
notes of life sing clear
as I find sweet refuge
in this graceful abode.
Hurricanes can devour
a form in great rage,
but nothing touches
the eyes that I dwell in,
A quaint cottage turned
into heaven's kingdom,
so long as I remain open
to feel your essence
connecting with mine.

Jeffrey Vionito, 39, Dallas, Texas

Positive Affirmations

I am Safe

I am Loved

I am Secure

I am a Divine Being who is perfectly Protected and lovingly Guided

I am a Child of God

I Love and I am Loved unconditionally

I am Grounded and Rooted here on this Earth and I have nothing to fear

I am Content with what I have and know that the Universe will provide me with everything I need.

The Sacral Chakra (Svadhisthana)

The sacral chakra is located at the naval area and is originally known as *Svadhisthana* in Sanskrit meaning 'Sacred Home of Self.' It deals with the fun and playful aspects of our lives and represents the Inner Child. It allows us to experience our true desires.

As young children, we are meant to feel safe and free and have a sense of playfulness and enjoyment. We are free to explore what excites us and brings enjoyment. We feel safe and loved and free to explore the world around us and trust our own instincts, abilities and talents. However as we grow older these beliefs can be 'undone' through negative messages we receive creating fear in our own abilities, creativity and sense of enjoyment.

The sacral chakra is linked to our sense of taste. It is our 'taste' for the world and thirst for freedom and pleasure that enlivens us. This chakra is also associated with vitality, virility, sexuality and pleasure; it represents the sweet exchange of connectedness and intimacy. The sacral chakra depicts our emotional consciousness or our 'animal instincts.' It represents the mammalian portion of our brain where the limbic system rules our emotions and short-term memory. The limbic system is an important centre for creativity and learning because it is where emotion and memory combine.

When this centre is blocked, we feel deadened or numb to that which should bring us joy or passion; we lack creativity, the freedom to feel safe to play as well as loss of sex drive. We may also experience fear or guilt associated with sex, sensuality or sexuality and become overly concerned with a sense of responsibility and duty to distract ourselves from exploring and enjoying the world around us creatively.

When it is overactive, we may form unhealthy attachments or addictions to sex, drugs, alcohol, food and even people. We may make rash decisions, jump into fast-moving relationships to compensate for a void inside. When the centre is clear, we experience a healthy balance between experiencing things that bring us pleasure and joy. When the sacral chakra is balanced, we feel at one with our Self and safe to experience the profound beauty of the world as well as express ourselves creatively. We experience a passion for life and our feelings flow freely.

This chakra represents ages 2-4 years old. Emotional events that occur during this age are often not conscious of the adult Self, but they form the basis of many of our core beliefs about ourselves and our abilities.

Orange

Orange is a passionate and vibrant colour associated with creativity, joy, passion and zest for life and excitement. It is a mixture of an energetic and fiery red and a joyful yellow forming a tantalising and flamboyant colour in its own right. This colour bursts with energy and brightness, and uplifts the spirit. Unlike the physical reaction of red and mental reaction of yellow, orange relates to 'gut reaction.' It appeals to our Inner Child and bounces us into action.

Scientific evidence suggests that it is an emotionally uplifting colour and helps to overcome grief, disappointment and loss. It relates to our sense of spontaneity and motivation and, like red, also stimulates the appetite. It is said to increase the level of oxygen to the brain and stimulate mental activity that increases inspiration.

In heraldry orange represents strength and endurance. Too much orange can over stimulate and overwhelm the brain and senses making it difficult to 'switch off.'

- **Dark orange:** can denote manipulation, distrust or deceit.
- **Red-orange:** represents desire, sexuality, excitement, motivation, pleasure, aggression and domination
- **Gold:** The meaning of gold is illumination, wisdom, and wealth. It evokes the feeling of prestige and often symbolizes high quality.

'*Orange is the happiest colour.*' — Frank Sinatra[3]

---

[3] **Francis Albert 'Frank' Sinatra** (December 12, 1915 – May 14, 1998)was an American singer and film actor most famous for singing New York New York

THE EYE

You gave me the eye the other night.
Looked me down hard.
The air between us cracked for a hot moment
with a bolt of ambiguous desire.

I was struck,
became helplessly flustered.

Grew flushed and wanting.

You sauntered by me,
your chest puffed out meaningfully in my direction,
projecting rough masculinity like a magnet
that you know has the power
to draw me in.

If only time, distance, and social decorum
did not stand in the way,
I would have cut the space between us in two
with the sharpness of my fierce and unceasing heart,
rained a torrent of kisses on your lips
and unleashed the wiles of my native passion upon your body
like a ferocious and tender storm.

Tamara Malya,

RIVERPOOL

my life is like a riverpool a movin' mighty fast
i'm known to skip a beat or two - won't nothin' never last?
if i should fall in love with you, please tell me if it's true
cause i can't tell the difference now that i made love to you

my life is like a riverpool a pullin' me along
i'm known to skip a beat or two when the feelin's really strong
if i should fall in love with you don't drown me by the quay
my life is like a riverpool a draggin' me away

E. Lee Caleca, 63, Tennessee, USA

UNTITLED

I walked a lonely road,
Not knowing who I am,
Lost in the wilderness,
A bubble in this God forsaken land.
I buckled to empty promises,
Gave away self as easy as sin,
Not knowing how to love myself,
I gave up and gave in.
My woman my man suffered,
Destructive my inner self was left to pay,
As I compromised my soul for flesh driven ways.
I never knew my promise,
My posture certainly wasn't straight,
And as I sit here perplexed
I knew I needed a time for change.
It's easy to lose value,
On oneself if you don't know who you are,
And if you are not taught how to love yourself,
Your flesh's desires can become addictive
In a world where we are disillusioned by an ungodly persona.

We then grow and become the issue,
Of a lost generation, prisoners within our own skin,
Our spirits now suffered and left isolated,
As our flesh develops the belief to win.

A TIME FOR CHANGE IS NEEDED

Darren Moxam, 35, London, England

I WANT TO LOOK AT YOU AND REMEMBER

I want to look at you and remember what it is like
To fall in love.
I want to drown in those brown eyes of yours,
Those endless pools of chocolate
Of honey darkened with desire.
I want butterflies to wreak havoc inside my stomach
And flutter all the way
Into my naked soul.

I want to look at you and remember what it is like
To be in love.
I want to recall those arms that delighted to
Wrap themselves around me.
Those arms
That wrapped up my body
And fit as snugly as a
Surgeon's glove.

I want to look at you and remember what it is like
To be loved
To be beheld as a queen
With extraordinary beauty
To be kissed by a man as if starved
As if, tongue parched,
Craves for Water
That is I.

I want to remember.
I want to remember.
I cannot bear to forget.

Wakonyo A Gachanja, 21, Nairobi , Kenya

Positive Affirmations

I am a creative being who enjoys exploring all the wonderful things the world has to offer

My zest for life is limitless

I create my own enjoyment

I am passionate about discovering new and exciting opportunities

I embrace opportunities to have fun and play

I embrace my sexuality and am comfortable and complete

I enjoy expressing my innermost desires and needs in an intimate relationship

Solar Plexus (Manipura)

The solar plexus chakra is known as *manipura* in Sanskrit which means 'city of jewels.' It is the central base for our personal power. It relates to self-esteem, 'warrior energy' and transformation of power and our ability to get up and go. I envision this as the flame inside us that keeps us centred within our own power and purpose. It is our fighting spirit that keeps us alive and is linked to the personality and social identity of the individual including self-worth and purpose. It rules how well we can maintain our sense of Self when in a power struggle with another.

When the *manipura* is balanced, we have a strong sense of identity, self-worth and purpose. We are able to value and learn from experiences. The *manipura* controls our mental thought and when balanced, functions healthily, allowing us to consciously have control over our thoughts, words and actions instead of just reacting to others.

When it is weak or blocked, the person may experience feelings of powerlessness, helplessness and loss of identity. Blockages are usually caused by the transference of negative energies of others. This can manifest itself in negative self-talk or the replication of negative messages we received as children which has created a lack of self-worth, self-belief and esteem.

When this chakra is overactive, we may become controlling of others or feel that we need to consistently take care of others by becoming overinvolved in their lives.

This chakra represents our sense of sight and our mental thought rather than emotional. It also characterises ages 6 - adolescence, a time when our sense of belonging switches from family to friends as well as a period where we are beginning to find and establish our place in the world.

Yellow

Yellow is a bright, bold and illuminating colour that represents our intellectual mind and thought. It symbolises acquired knowledge, teaching and learning and which resonates with the left or logic side of the brain stimulating our mental ability, perception and ability to recall information and analyse. It is a vibrant colour that radiates at a high frequency which can stimulate new ideas and ways of thinking but can also create anxiety and cause the individual to overanalyse and become critical.

Yellow is a radiant and joyful colour and represents youth. Just like the sun, it symbolises happiness, optimism and energy. It is used to grab people's attention and stimulate the brain. Yellow also symbolises the need to exercise caution. It is the colour that lies between red and green - a point at which we must stop, reflect and discern.

In heraldry, yellow is associated with honour and loyalty, however, after a period of time has come to represent cowardice and dishonour. Yellow is used for mourning in Egypt and actors of the Middle Ages wore yellow to signify the dead. Traditionally, yellow ribbons were worn as a sign of hope as women waited for their men to come home from war. Yellow has also represented courage (Japan), merchants (India), and peace.

Dark yellow: can denote decay, sickness, treachery, deceit, cowardice, low self-esteem.

Bright Yellow: optimism, joy, happiness, courage, hope..

'There are painters who transform the sun to a ***yellow*** *spot, but there are others who with the help of their art and their intelligence, transform a* ***yellow*** *spot into sun.'*

— Pablo Picasso[4]

---

[4] **Pablo Ruiz y Picasso**, was a Spanish painter, sculptor, printmaker, ceramicist, stage designer, poet and playwright. He was the co-founder of Cubism.

ODE TO BILLY

That man has consumed my brain
Has me elated and forlorn
And all within the blink of an eye
That man is no good for me
Yet everything I ever wanted
Fills me with purpose
And leaves me lacking
Need to shake him off
But want him to shake me down
Want him to fuck off
But come on home
That man makes me stutter when I talk
And blush when I walk, beside him
Has me all hot inside
Legs open wide
To welcome him in
He has me questioning my sanity
Justifying my feelings
Forgetting to work, forgetting to breathe
Breathe.... out and release
That man has me giggling like a school girl
Whilst doubting my womanly beauty
What kind of man is this?
That man is no good for me....
But.....
But.....
But whatever he is.
I'm his.
Forever more

Tasha Janine, 44, London, UK

REWRITTEN SOUL

I opened up my Soul to you
Left it exposed to the naked eye
You opened the door, curious
And inspected the contents of I

At first you circled it, delicately
Treading ever so softly
Skirted around my **True** content
And inspected the content of I

Like a moth to a flame, my Brightness enticed you
Attracted to such light
Yet unwilling to See its origins
Or why I shone so bright

Eyes closed for so many years
Shut tight to Who I really Be
Too complex and three dimensional
So blind you could not See

Threatened you searched for a light switch
To drain away the 'excess' energy
A switch, a plug, a wire
To erase it from my memory

Not content somehow you penetrated me
At night you climbed into my skin
and sat upon
my Soul

Left your marks and scars and pains
Upon my bloody wrists
Tied tight were chains

Lost, forgotten and troubled Spirit
Origins covered with layer upon layer of Fat
From his arse
I use to grab with delight

Swept under the carpet
Slicked back tight
Like nappy hair with a strong scent of unnatural chemicals
HER STORY no longer bears relevance

Masked, taped and filed away
Into the 'miscellaneous' cabinet

Daniella Blechner, 34 London, UK

ODE AD AVIUM (ODE TO BIRDS)

There's a yellow-bird that became
ground years ago in my backyard.
He still flies — I see him in dreams sometimes;
flying high and low—in between the two extremes;
cage-free,
How he was meant to be.
A decade behind bars,
His song couldn't even break thro' them–
If he were to know of the freedom
as above so below would his soul still glow
with sonata? His parting was unexpected
as dying almost always is,
But it was a blessing–
For wingéd fellows all fine and yellow
are small sky people only to occasionally
be partially encased by conjoined twigs,
fully temporarily enveloped in brittle shell to begin,
Meant for a forever friendship with Aether.
Little canary, please forgive me for I have sinned,
Sweet angel I'm happy you have escaped
from your involuntary jailbird fate,
For as long as I live I'll appreciate
what is beautiful, let it be
Without taking it for myself 'til
it withers and leaves but a tiny sun-hued feather
covered by dirt and decaying leaves and freshly fallen snow.
We're birds too
if we want to be,
Little do we know…

Eva Xanthopoulos, 24, Cleveland, USA

OBITUARY OF MY UNMARRIED SELF

Till death, till death,
till death do us part.
Parts of me died
on our wedding day.
I sobbed
on our wedding day.
Overwhelmed? Overjoyed?
No.
Mourning
parts severed, parts rendered,
parts fractured, strewn, destroyed.

All that I am
I give to you.
No.
All that I was
I gave to you, gave to you.
Once I was strong;
Fierce in love, valiant in laughter,
Resolved
in clenching myself
in my fist forever.
What use is a steely grip,
when that self
has gone to ether?

I honour you,
I respect you,
I comfort you,
I protect you.
Hell, I even love you – intensely.

let none, but marriage,
put us asunder
so long as we both shall live,
shall live, shall live.

Our vows
were not murderous,
Our vows
were casked
in an institution
that sprays power
indiscriminately;
like a desperate child
with a semi-automatic
on a killing spree;
which all should uphold and honour, honour.
Uphold
and kill tenderly,
with honour.

Natalie Brinham, Malaysia

DISAPPEARING ACT

I surrendered to your love
You said you couldn't resist – me
You said you wanted – me – that I was 'special',
New, yet familiar, I got wrapped up in your arms

I yearned for your touch; I lapped your love right up
For I so enjoyed your kisses all over my body
from lips, hips, toes, back to lips
leaving no place untouched

I relished as you caressed my
sensitive parts
I moaned, I swore as I opened
myself completely to your body

As you entered me and loved me
continuously for a whole two hours on my special day
You left – me – and I felt so wonderful
on my birthday – it was high noon

I was not expecting to not see you later
on this day of all days
Slowly, I cotton on, not wanting to at first
as you reveal a side I don't know

You eventually show, but won't tell
of why you abandoned ship
you seem to be messing with my mind
as I fathom, and try to find

Instead, I end up bemused,
confused and finally

disappointment settles right in
I process my thoughts on my own

Your disappearing act
was unfriendly at best
silence took a hold
and for two whole days I couldn't rest

Eventually you send words
you mention something about
your humble apologies
which releases tears of pain, for I refused to cry until then

When you show up in the flesh
You refuse to explain -
you seem to be on some other weird and
strange plane

For my hurt feelings
seem to frighten you away
and I learn the hard way
that you're emotionally unavailable

You duck and dive
Not taking on my feelings
Gazing out of the window
you say you are in limbo

Eventually there is acceptance
but the seeds of mistrust have been sown
Now I see you in a different light
Without truth, there is no future with you

Sadness has now arrived
as I know the love we had
cannot proceed without openness
it won't survive the course

And as the love fades
I guard my feelings
and keep my distance
things will never be the same again

I've so enjoyed being loved by you
But not being loved by you
feels lonely
And I've lost that loving feeling

No more judgements
No more expectations
I refuse to let you hurt me ever again
I refuse to let you drain my spirit

I re-learn though, that I'm well capable
of love and I look forward to sharing
that beautiful experience
with Mr emotionally available – I'm ready!

Nicole, 60, London, England

INTO THE ARMS OF THE BRUTAL MAN

He raises his voice, he cannot just discuss
the issues between them, he has to curse,
he hits her so bad, she needs a nurse,
yet she never leaves him despite it getting worse.

She gives him love, he repays her with pain,
she always tries to please him, but he will always complain,
love has blinded her; that is why she will remain,
in that so called relationship that is extremely insane.

I look into her eyes so cold and empty,
and I reach out to touch all so gently,
because it's been ages since she had a touch so friendly,
because all his touches are nothing short of deadly.

Oh how I wish. . .
I could punch him in the face,
for all his shame and utter disgrace,
oh how I wish,
he was a memory that I could erase,
so she wouldn't have to remember that mental case.

Oh how I wish. . .
there was something that could be done,
to make sure that he causes her no more harm,
but it is all just hopeless wishing in the long run,
because from her experiences she still cannot learn,
she will not leave him, sadly she will always return,
into the arms of that brutal man.

Emmanuel Kariuki, 24, Nairobi, Kenya

GRADE SCHOOL CURRICULUM

We really weren't taught how to do the important things
Like how to be happy in your own skin
Appreciate the package in which we came
Because no matter how we try who we are truly remains the same
How to accept sadness and grief and move on from it
As with life comes death and with or without us it goes on
How to get over a broken heart and disappointment
Because as long as there is love hearts will break
How to be selfless not selfish
As the moral code is relevant even if we don't get our way
How to appreciate that all the rights one believes he has the other person has too
That the most important thing in life is life itself.

Simone Dunbar, Kingston, Jamaica

Positive Affirmations

I am perfectly balanced and in control

I forgive and release anyone who I feel may have taken my power at any time

I am strong and know exactly what I want and how to express what I need

I create clear and consistent boundaries in my day to day life

I am able to listen to other's opinions and feelings without fear of criticism or attack

I am a Child of God who deserves to be loved, honoured and acknowledged

I define who I am at all times. I am my own judge who lovingly guides my Soul onto the right track without judgement or fear.

My feelings are important and I must pay them the utmost respect so others will too

The Heart Chakra

(Anahata)

The heart chakra is the first of the higher vibrational chakras and is located at the centre of our breastbone or sternum. It is the link between our internal selves and the eternal Universe and others. It is linked to our sense of touch and represents the stage of adolescence (a time when we tend to rebel against those who have loved us). It is associated with unconditional love and kindness.

The heart chakra seeks a harmonious relationship and sense of 'connectedness' with the world around us; it radiates and recognises the love that resides in all living beings. It acts as a vessel that connects all our other chakras together and unlike the first three chakras, is less concerned with survival, emotions, power and individualism, and more with compassion for humankind as a collective.

The heart chakra represents the balance between power,

love and wisdom. It is the centre point where our feminine and masculine energies meet. The fourth chakra rules all of our inter- and intra-personal relationships and is primarily concerned with our perception of love as well as our ability to give and receive love.

Our heart chakras are divided into two parts: our 'Lower Heart' and our 'High Heart.' Our Lower Heart deals with love on a human level whereas our High Heart rules unconditional love and compassion for all sentient beings. Human love can be filled with negativity, fear, jealousy and anger whereas unconditional love is a selfless appreciation and compassion for another being; a recognition that they, too are a Soul, on a journey who, like us, has the ability to love unconditionally. 'The Love in me salutes the Love in you.'

'*It is the challenge of our hearts to connect with and receive the love of our spiritual SELF so that we can heal the harm that others have done to us. Then, from the heart space of healing and self-love, we can love others as well.*'-Suzanne Caroll (www.multidimension.com)

When our heart chakra is balanced, we are able to give and receive love healthily; we are able to demonstrate loving kindness to others without a desire for a 'return.' We are also able to experience, joy, self-love, acceptance and fulfilment. Our lives are full of joy without judgement or a need to control.

When our heart chakra is too open, we may become jealous, possessive and love with conditions.

When our heart chakra is blocked, we may be holding onto past hurts, unable to forgive. We may be carrying bitterness, grief and so feelings of blame and anger towards those who deem to have hurt us. We may become jealous, angry, controlling or even shut ourselves off from love by building walls around our hearts. We may feel unworthy of receiving love, fear rejection, abandonment or find it difficult to express love due to past hurts. These past hurts stop us from moving forward into a love we deserve. The key to a balanced heart chakra is to forgive ourselves, as well as others and let go.

Jonah and the Whale

The story of Jonah and the whale, regardless of faith, carries a powerful message to all.

The account opens with God speaking to Jonah, son of Amittai. He instructs him to go to the city of Nineveh and preach repentance. Jonah 1:2 '*Arise, go to Nineveh the great city and cry against it, for their wickedness has come up before Me*.'

Jonah found this order impossible and decided, instead to flee. He went down to the seaport of Joppa and climbed aboard a ship to Tarshish. The opposite direction to Nineveh!

Soon after, a terrible storm descended upon them and the ship was tossed from side to side. Jonah, believing he was responsible for the storm as a result of God's anger, begged the people aboard the ship to toss him over. They did what he asked and the storm calmed.

Instead of drowning, Jonah was swallowed by an enormous whale where he was left repenting and begging for forgiveness for three days. He praised God proclaiming, 'Salvation comes from the Lord!' (Jonah 2:9)

God commanded the whale to vomit the reluctant prophet onto the land. This time, Jonah, the anti-hero, obeyed. He entered the city of Nineveh preaching repentance. He said that if they did not repent then God would destroy their city within 40 days. They listened to Jonah's message and changed their ways. Peace was restored.

However, rather than be pleased that the people had changed and the city was restored to a place of peace, Jonah was angry that God had not punished them.

I call this attitude 'mercy for me, justice for them.' He did not see that they too, were children of God who deserved forgiveness and peace, just as he. This story strikes a huge chord with me. It conveys a God who is compassionate and forgiving rather than one who is angry and vengeful. And so this links to the heart chakra by reinforcing the message that we must desire mercy not just for ourselves but for all. Releasing our bitterness or our desire for punishment against those who may have harmed us allows us to give and receive love healthily- to love and be loved.

Green

Green is the colour of life. It signifies a fresh energy and natural living. It symbolises regeneration, rebirth and revitalisation. It is the colour of Spring; a time when fresh life springs anew and endings bring on new beginnings. Green is the colour of our natural environment. It is the colour of the heart chakra which exudes love and therefore is often used to depict professions related to care and service such as nurses, healers, counsellors and charities. Conversely, green can represent money, wealth and prosperity. In America, it is the colour of money. These two contrasting ideas of service and prosperity make green a colour of perfect harmony and balance.

From a colour psychology standpoint, it is the balance between the head and the heart. Green consists of two polar opposites; blue and yellow. It perfectly blends the cool, calm and collective qualities of blue and dynamism and mental stimulation of yellow. The contrasts within this colour make green an excellent colour of balance and good judgement. Green represents the ability to make good decisions based equally from the head and the heart. Green represents positivity, peace and unconditional love and is therefore a perfect colour to stimulate a sense of calm.

Universally, green is the colour for 'go' and in heraldry represents, growth and hope. Green is the national colour for Ireland (The Emerald Isle) and is a religious colour for Irish Catholics. This colour is also a religious colour for Islam and represents the prophet Mohammed. Did you know in China it is a disgrace to give a man a green hat because it indicates that his wife is cheating on him?

Yellow green: sickly, cowardice and weakness.

Dark green: ambition, greed, resentment, wealth.

Emerald green: inspirational, uplifting, abundance and youth.

'*Green is the prime colour of the world, and from that which all loveliness arises.*'

— *Pedro Calderón de la Barca*[5]

[5] **Pedro Calderón de la Barca y Barreda González de Henao Ruiz de Blasco y Riaño,** usually referred as Pedro Calderón de la Barca, was a dramatist, poet and writer of the Spanish Golden Age

MS INDEPENDENT

In her eyes you see strength
A woman who's trod a rocky road
At times she felt she was never going to make it
But marched on and carried her load

Never asked a soul for anything
Strings of let-downs and disappointments taught her to mistrust
Yet she is the Go-To woman
Her advice and Love is a must
But who was there for her, in her darkest hour when she lay in bed alone?
Who was there for Ms Independent at the other end of a phone?

Dependent only on herself
Yet others depend on her
Can pay her bills and keep her home
Hold down a job and feed her kids alone
And still have cash to lend a friend

Ever the Independent woman- seemingly happy and content
She is the Go-To woman: the glue, the fix, the cement
has a smile for everyone and everything, friends, family and those unknown
Everyone thinks she has her s**t in order
Nobody sees her at night- alone

Provider and protector to those who depend on her
Yet do you see her silent tears?
Her sadness or her deepest fears?
Do you see beyond her head held high?
Her broken heart or teary eyes?

Do you know the pain within?
See her world or where she's been?

Eloquent at offering advice to others
Yet struggles to take her own
Excellent friends, sisters and mothers
But misses a man in her home

Never take this woman's kindness for weakness
She is made of serious stuff
Her kindness is a reflection of her spirit
She'll share and give even when she has not enough
This isn't because she is weak; it's because inside her she only has Love

Don't take this woman at face value
See beyond the smile
Spend time to find out her story
And listen to her for a while

Even when times were tough, she struggled on for she had not a choice
She learnt to depend on herself and listen to her Inner voice
Even in her darkest hour
When things got bad and things got sour
She pulled herself up and said, 'Never again!'
In saying this she branded all men
They take, they use, they drain, they leave
She learnt that it's not just in death you grieve

'Never Again!' she cried inside
As she spoke these words, part of her died
And she built a wall surrounding her heart
The barriers of self-protection
An undeniable vow- Till Death Do We Part
Her armour replaced her affection

The Independent woman is a beauty to behold
Envied by many from the outside looking in
But scratch beyond the surface
You'll simply find a woman who yearns to be loved from outside and within
To be treated kindly and with respect
To be acknowledged and appreciated
To have someone who understands
To comfort her both In the day and at night
To have a companion to hold her hand
And tell **her** 'everything is alright.'

Independent Woman keep strong; it's how we've been raised and been grown
But don't be afraid to drop those bags- we don't need to suffer alone.

Daniella Blechner, 34, London, UK

JILTED...

At the crossroad we met
and it was just you and I
that followed this Road,
As soon as we started,
being a novice, I confessed
I had never followed such a Road.
But I felt angel led
I followed behind you
and behold together we trod
along this stretched, flowery Road
save for the few curves and thorny bushes
that once or twice we encountered.
And countless miles into the Road
you, all suddenly,

Disappeared

And I not a single idea I had
as to why you abandoned me
at such a point in this Road
where it was all thorny and curved.
And even as I struggle hard
lonely and betrayed,
at least I sight the crossroad
Word has it that you now have Richard
way into a similar Road
only a day after my ordeal.
And I wonder why Fate could be so wicked
even to hurt people so humbled.
And when I reach the crossroad,
I'll follow the other road.

Babbou Nicholas, 21, Kisii, Kenya

RELATIONSHIP CYCLE FLAWS

Imagine feeling like whenever you get close to someone
your mind and body wants to separate,
your body is open to them
but your mind doesn't want to open up that way.
You enjoy their company as a friend
but when it comes to commitments,
those actions your soul doesn't comprehend.

You make excuses why you can't be together
deep down knowing the main reason is you,
a past that haunts not allowing you to prosper,
cheating and mistrust the bad seeds
and the reason to why you do the things you do.
You tell yourself you'd prefer a life of emptiness
instead of confronting these issues,
then loneliness appears as your confusion
combined with fear not knowing what to do.
You ask God to change your insides
desperately needing to renew your mind,
yet when this situation reappears
you remain caught up in that time.

Imagine lusting after the thought of being loved
but whenever close it seems to run away,
and the more you want it
it never shows you the right of way.
Your soul is at a loss
and all you feel is despair,
loneliness the reality
accompanied by tears.
In desperation you get caught up in false promises

relationships that are not healthy for your insides,
mixed emotions, mixed messages,
confused by the emotional rollercoaster of life.

Relationship Cycle Flaws,
Diluted truth,
Empty promises of heart's content
leads towards disappointment,
in oneself and others.
You had me caught up, I believed, just didn't see
we were not meant to be, but now I know
how do I go on, when I trust no more.
They created mistrust in us
and all of the above,
Now we are caught up
in a cycle of non-believers.
Insecurity leading towards possessive acts,
Checking of the phone,
Questions, always wondering where your partner is at,
Not knowing all along
you are driving your partner in that direction.
The one where mistrust is placed,
The one where the belly of the beast's haven lays,
Questions, driving his or her mind to stray,
They are now wondering will something better come their way.
A man or woman who really cares,
Beyond man made disillusioned acts
where your mind is constantly at,
Believing your thoughts as the truth,
Driving his or her sanity insane
because of trust issues.
Until they reach the final point of relationship flaws,
A break-up now manifests,

Darren Moxam, 35, London, England

THE BLEMISHED RESISTANCE

He was an over thinking boy,
She was a spontaneous girl,
Two unfamiliar persons,
With an incredible bond.

He lacked light in his life,
And so was always hit by the huge, unexpected raindrops of life,
She never knew safety,
And so was always looking for a safe haven to escape to.

She kept everything inside,
Just as a broken wall covered with a painting appears,
He was semi-porous,
Just needing trust as the activating agent for his emotions to be released, and for him to receive others.

He was aware but unaware of how to deal,
She was unaware but aware of how to respond,
But both were sealed with inevitability.

With timing unknown,
They found each other,
But it seemed that the bed of roses had thorns,
Although these thorns were too brittle for their now
'Blemished Resistance'

His nagging sense of insecurity became a past illusion,
Her Berlin Wall of emotion tumbled down like a mud house.

He, all of a sudden could walk through the rain untouched,
And she found a rock to cling onto even as the wind attempted to blow her away.

For both,
Their resistance against acceptance was blemished,
Blemished by the purest and rarest substance,
Love was it,
Resistance was blemished by Love.

Mercy Teko, 18 Nairobi, Kenya

I AM GRASS

now I am grass
our paths cross along some deep ash beach
you are here to swim with the turtles
i am here to do a little kingdom building of my own
our eyes met and then I drift away
as detestable as my own selfishness
if only I could stay
i am numb and comfortable
budgeting my life against time
my lack of peace transparent
i think you must have many
but maybe I'm the one
i am more enclosed in memory than process
shadowed by my past
i want to stay but then I drift away
voices far on the crest of the ocean scream for me
taking my distress
for a second I am anchored
but greed is a cunning hunter
crushing my spirit
taking in trade what is valuable to my heart
leaving it fallow ground
plow in me whatever you wish
the seed will not stick
i am bad soil
a portrait of brokeness
worlds away from who I was to be
you burn into me like the excess of thieves
forcing me to genius
and for a moment
I am grass

E. Lee Caleca, 63. Tennessee, USA

MY HEART IS RESTORED

One by one
Day after day
I slowly picked up the pieces
Each one so very precious.

I put them together carefully
Making sure each was in the right place
Now that they are together again
They are restored.

Again, in their rightful place
Made whole again
To be treasured
Filled with immeasurable joy
My heart!

By Simone Dunbar, Kingston, Jamaica

ENOUGH

Today I'm fighting urges,
Weakness maybe,
A tender heart
Wanting to be loved.
I miss you,
Still care for you,
Love you.
My heart can't let go
So easily,
Though my mind,
Convinced otherwise,
Pulls me further away.
I love you but I know,
I must accept the truth--
Love is not enough
For me and you.

Ghada Khoraych, 31, Toronto, Canada

I FORGOT TO LOVE ME

Currently there's a woman who walks around with her head down
Currently there's a woman that is always wearing a frown
There's a woman that looks in the mirror everyday...
And sees minor things that she wants to change
There's a woman that others feel are so beautiful
But the one she truly loved was so critical
You see....
She was constantly trying to please
Constantly trying to fulfil his every need
For him she would do anything
She loved him so much ... treated him like a king
But that one cold day when he decided to leave...
All alone and broken hearted with added low self esteem
She said to herself....
I forgot to love ME

Tyraa Nicole Caldwell, 30, Redford, Michigan

HOW DO I LOVE ME LIKE A ROSE?

How do I love me, like a Rose Blossom
Let me count the ways, in my song of praise
I love me to the depth of my soul
Soul soft as a petal, spirit glides
Into my mind, body the trinity, one whole
In this bright beautiful vessel it prides
The head and the temples fragrant role
I love me blossoming and dignified.
A spring erection, crimson like blood flows
In battle against killers: winter storms
Choking weeds, petal pickers. A cut Rose
Buds and grows, soft yet strong arm of thorns.
How do I love me, beautiful flower?
Red Rose I affirm self-love is power

Amanda Epe, London, England

HOW DO I LOVE THEE? HAIKUS

"How do I love Thee?"
To receive pure love, at first
Sight I must love me

"How do I Love Thee?"
No condition, first love me
Then you, one mission

"How do I love Thee?"
You are my king, I adore
Requited to Queen

Amanda Epe, London, England

YOU AND YOU AND YOU

The best advice
Previously not taken
Now fills my ears
Infiltrates my brain
"Like attracts like"
Disarm the old ways
Release the ties
Of people not worthy
I am talking about you
And you and you and you
All of the toxicity
And the only blame is me
For the power is deep
Within my soul
Searching for truth
As they fall in the cracks
But it's up to me to exercise
All of them
Who try to bleed me dry
As I let it all go
So to you, and you, and you
Who think you know me
I tell you, you know me the least
As I watch you pass by
And smile as I let you walk by
Your chin down, realizing what you lost
But that is of no consequence
To me who knows the real truth
Your loss is my gain
Getting rid of what holds me down
To my true magnificence
As I'm the real winner

Rachel, USA

Positive Affirmations

My heart is open and I am free to Love

I am open to give and receive Love.

I acknowledge myself as a beautiful being of Light and I Love myself and reflect this Love unselfishly to others

Love flows freely to me and I acknowledge and accept that I am surrounded by Love

Love exists in everything I see. Every flower, every tree, every animal, every plant and everyone is lovingly created and nurtured. I lovingly remove the blocks in my mind and in my heart so that I may accept and receive this Love now

I am Loved . I Love. I am Love

Only Love is real

The Throat Chakra (Vishuddha)

VISHUDDHA
throat chakra

The throat chakra is located at the base of the throat area and represents communication and self-expression. It symbolises the ability to express and voice our dreams. *Vishuddha* in Sanskrit means 'pure place.' Contrary to the name, the throat chakra, or Vishuddha, represents the sense of hearing. In order to speak our Truths, we must *hear* our inner guidance system before we speak it.

When the throat chakra is clear, we are able to form positive relationships people as we are able to communicate and express ourselves clearly. A clear throat chakra enables us to express ourselves without fear of criticism or what others may think. This allows us to form healthy relationships based on truthful communication and true intimacy.

When it is blocked, we may have difficulty expressing ourselves and our opinions. We may stammer or stutter or sometimes, not even voice our truths at all. We may become static, blocked and uninspired leading to a lack of creativity and poor communication with others. A blocked chakra can be caused by a fear of speaking out, belief that other's views are more important or repressed emotions such as guilt, shame or anger. Symptoms can manifest themselves physically in the form of a sore throat, coughing or stuttering.

An overactive throat chakra signifies a person who can be too opinionated and dominant; the person can be judgemental or over critical of others. They may shout a lot, not allow others to express their opinions or even be verbally abusive.

The throat chakra represents the stage of adulthood; a time when we are fully established in our sense of Self and are fully responsible for our communication with others. The key to a clear throat chakra is to seek our inner guidance and speak our Truths without fear of attack from others.

Blue

Blue is a calm and tranquil colour often giving a sense of clarity and transparency. It is the colour of the sky, ocean, sea and water and is therefore often used to represent freedom. This colour is also one of trust, honesty and loyalty. Blue is associated with trust and is often used in healthcare to represents cleanliness and hygiene. From a colour psychology perspective, blue is reliable and responsible. It gives a sense of confidence and inner security.

This colour also promotes tranquillity and peace; it reduces stress and enhances physical and mental relaxation. It is also proved to slow metabolism allowing a sense of inner peace and respite. Blue is the colour of freedom and self-expression; freedom to express and freedom to communicate.

Blue is a masculine colour that also depicts stability and security and in heraldry, blue is used to symbolize piety and sincerity. Traditionally, Greeks believe that the colour blue wards off 'The Evil Eye'. On the other hand, in Korea it is the colour of mourning.

As much as blue is a calming, peaceful and stable colour, blue can often represent a sense of melancholy and depression. This is where the style of music known as *the blues* came from. The style originated and evolved in African communities primarily within the 'Deep South' of the United States in the early 19th century.

- **Pale Blue:** Freedom, peace, tranquillity, softness, calm.
- **Turquoise:** clarity of thought, communication, energy, serenity.
- **Dark Blue:** responsibility, security, stability, knowledge, power and integrity.

'*The blues is an expression of anger against shame and humiliation.*'

— B B King[6]

[6] B B King is an African American Blues singer, songwriter and guitarist well known for singing 'Thrill Is Gone', 'How Blue Can You Get?' and 'Sweet Little Angel.'

LOVE'S LANGUAGE

How do I tell you that I love you
When the words "I love you" are so played out?
I love sunsets; I love my Jimmy Choos,
And I love a cool breeze during summer
blowing in from the south.
I love good chocolate, feeling silk and people-watching on the train,
I love honesty, Italian food and London in the rain.
But when it comes to you...
Love doesn't justify or quantify,
I can say the words, but they still won't qualify
As an explanation for these feelings I have for you.
The conclusion that I've reached is it's not what you say but what you do.
It's the look behind your eyes I see which makes me feel desired,
It's the nourishment you feed into my soul when it gets tired.
It's the compromise you make when reason's heading out of town,
It's the way you make me happy when the world has made me frown.
And so
My Love's language it would seem has no lyrics, no sound, no volume,
The voice of your love is action, so let your deeds become your anthem.

LOVE'S SOUNDTRACK

While it's true, the word love is over-used, and this has
watered down its meaning.
Love does have a sound, a tone, a vibe, even a leaning.
The sound is your lover's heartbeat as they're lying in your
arms,
Then, of course, the sound of laughter as they are lost inside
your charms.
Not empty declarations or half promises, borne of cynical
agenda,
Or unoriginal clichéd lines that have your ears screaming
"return to sender."
The sound of love is communication, some silent, some loud
as
an explosion,
The whisper of a thrill or the rush of a radical notion.
Feel the sound of my love, forget words but listen closely,
With your head, your hands, your eyes but I'd suggest your
heart mostly.
I agree that talk is cheap and actions speak a thousand
words,
But love deserves a soundtrack that every heart should say
it's heard.

Lawrence Coke, 38, London, England

SPEAK UP

I
was afraid
to speak the Truth of my Soul
Like a mouse I was afraid of my own voice
I stuttered, I spluttered, I shut down, I stammered
Enamoured with the words of others I forgot to honour my
own
Inside my mind were words of others and stories and
feelings unexpressed, and-
somewhere, within, this poem
I journeyed within to magical lands, travelled across all
space and time in my mind
In the darkness of my awareness, imagined words
unexpressed, feelings repressed
Tumbling from my mind to the recipient's chest
Yet in the stark light of day, I couldn't find a way
to express the feelings trapped inside
I would choke on my words and in my throat formed a knot
So I rehearsed in my mind
Use the most exquisite, eloquent words I could find
But deep inside there was a block
A bind inside my mind
That kept my tongue from loosening
I watched others in awe express their needs, wants and
desires
Unleash feelings into the air as easy as breathing
Writing came to me like a blessing
The pen-the bridge between my Soul's Truth and Expression
I was like a caged bird trapped in my own prison
Felt I'd so much to say with no one to listen
I buried my emotions and sunk into a pile of unrecognition

Today I stand loud and proud with something to say
We must honour our Truths and pave our own way
Without fear of rejection or what others may say
Nelson Mandela said it best when he said there's no pride in playing small
If we don't stand for anything we may fall for anything at all.

Daniella Blechner, 34, London, England

DOUBLE DUSK

In the depth of my slumber
I could make out an almost magical
figure from yonder,
An angel I thought,
But how orthodox of me to subscribe
to that school of thought.
Maybe it was because her dress hid her feet so that she
seemed to be hovering
above the ground,
One side of her dress danced to the
silent song of the wind,
And the other outlined her voluptuous
body.
The sun was sinking fast behind her,
Its sight momentarily blinding me.
Her rich exotic fragrance tickled my
nostrils even before I regained vision.
And there she was right before me,
An angel I had thought,
But now it didn't matter that she had no
wings,
That her eyes were brown not blue,
Her smile burst waves through me
more warmly than the rays of the sun
ever could.
I opened my mouth but not so much as
a whisper came out.
Of all days my larynx had chosen to
betray me then.
And as fast as she had come she was

headed back.
Deep wave of sadness engraved me
and I could hardly move,
And it didn't seem to help that the
overgrown roots seemed to swathe
my feet,
I could only see her posterior motion
silhouetted against the deep orange
sunset, an inch less with every blink
as she too sunk into the horizon.
Then came the breeze again,
this time I hoped it would be strong
enough to blow her back,
But all it did was blow past the dry
oak branches and made them creak,
A creak that sounded like a laugh, a
mock, a gibe.
TWICE I HAD SEEN THE SUN SET
THAT EVENING.

Denis, 20, Kenya

A crackle of electricity like distant applause
The familiar sound of a plaintive ring tone
The numbness leaves as nerves tingle
Both soloists clear throats and await their audience
Pause...
Silently, with the press of a finger the call is received
The first sound heard is a breath
The previous absence of sound- a sound in itself
A noticeable medley of blood pulsing through the ear
Seeking as if by osmosis to change life pulse into loquacious
speech.
Vibration struggling to find its pitch
Vocal cords hum to tune
Slowly, the first furtive words are spoken
An over rushed "hello" and its echo the first exchange.
A strange awkwardness chaffes against a most familiar
greeting.
The warmth in her voice, mellifluous and soothing sets the tone.
His serves as a sensitive hand to conduct the conversation.
Their tongues poised like conductors sticks
Orchestrating words to bring order to errant thoughts,
Which lurch staccato as breathe is drawn.
Formalities extended like out reaching hands,
A connection has been made.
They seek common ground on which to place their feet,
Suggestions made like Shuffling steps.
The rhythm and moment agreed,
Heralding the ushering in of the 1st movement.......
In time reviewers and critics will have their say..
Their words and actions a chorus line
.......to the eternal dance.

Jeff, London, England

THE DECLARATION

Upon every twinkle in the star-lit sky,
and every ticking of the clock passing by,
so sure is my heart that you're its delight;
I'm overwhelmed by emotions that overcome my might.
Just like the sun you light up my life,
and colour my world with your rainbow smile.
Though cloudy days have come and gone since the day you occurred,
love beats all odds to somehow cause the grey skies turn azure.

Upon every whistle of the wind in still night,
and every synchronized dance of the trees in musical delight,
so soothing is my darling's song to me,
besides Ludwig and Beethoven; my greatest symphony.
You've set my heart on fire,
indeed my heart is dire.
Walking away is no option,
not in a million years to come.
Because your love is mine and mine is yours,
until Kingdom come.

Winnie Wa Muhia, 24, Nairobi, Kenya

AN ARTIST IN LOVE

The painter
Boasts of her love for you in brush strokes
She captures the feeling in paint
And dazzles with colour
As she creates a perfect likeness of you
On canvas.

The dancer
Will train painstakingly
For each step, each move
Echoes her heartbeat
And how fiercely it beats for you.

The sculptor
Will love you with her hands
As she carves your replica
Out of soapstone
And leaves you breathless.

The singer
Will echo each perfect note
With her light, lilting voice
That sends your heart a-flutter
And she will wrap you in the warmth of song.

The writer
Will charm you with her flowery vocabulary
And narrate perfect love.
She'll flatter you with genius pun
And you'll find yourself in her grasp.

But I
I…
Will love you with my soul
Nothing more, nothing less.
The love of an artist.

Wakonyo A Gachanja , 21, Nairobi, Kenya

A LOVE SO NEAR BUT YET SO FAR

A love so near but yet so far;
is a love that connects the two. Brought by its reason of nonverbal reasoning yet it gives meaning without reason too!

A love so near but yet so far; is the adhesive for what makes it right to be wrong. For its purpose and intention allow time to stand still without motion just the beating of hearts ticking away. Confirming the motionless movement of time!

A love so near but yet so far; brings two people together although apart with cherished memories as the only evidence of their unseen existence. Only between the two can this type of encounter be circumvent!

A love so near but yet so far; can allow a smile to span from ear to ear at any given moment. Opening the forum for on lookers or not to question the sanity behind the mind-set of that person. Yet wish only for their own sanity to be questioned!!!

Only a love so near but yet so far; promotes two people who deserve to feel what they feel in this arena that sets them worlds apart. However, it's all encompassing expertise is timeless for they are simply. ' A part of the binary '
force that makes them whole!

Only a love so near but yet so far...

Diana Gray Lewis, London, England

Positive Affirmations

I am able to express myself clearly and coherently and what I have to say is valuable and important

I have a right to express myself and I do this without fear of what others may say or think about me

Today I realise that I have a message to spread and everyone can benefit from hearing my message

My words can heal or harm. I speak words in Truth and I choose to use words to heal

I clear the airways of my throat and shout from the top of my lungs, "I LOVE LIFE AND I INTEND TO EXPRESS AND COMMUNICATE WITH OTHERS IN A POSITIVE WAY!"

I can use my voice to Unite, Inspire and Empower people who have had their voice stripped away. Today I give a voice to the voiceless

My voice is a powerful tool that is designed to reach out and touch others with words in Love

Third Eye/Brow Chakra

(Ajna)

AJNA
The Third Eye Chakra

The brow chakra is beautiful indigo in colour and located in the centre of our forehead, between our eyes. The sixth and seventh chakras represent the expansion of our consciousness and spin at a faster rate than our lower chakras. The brow chakra is the window to our intuition and vision, and the link to a higher consciousness or state of being. The brow chakra, also known as the 'Third Eye', allows us to sense and feel the Truth, comprehend the motivations of others on a deeper level and acts as our Inner intuitive guide.

This chakra rules our imagination and vision and links to our spiritual views and beliefs. It is known as the 'Home of Spirit' and guides our dreams. Through our dreams we are able to explore our Outer worlds using our Inner Vision.

The brow chakra is linked to our 'sixth sense' and operates within the 85% of the brain we do not use. Through our dreams we are able to process past traumas, baggage and issues as well as heal and release. The brow chakra helps us to process the theatre of our lives and allows us to see beyond the two dimensional into what is really real in our lives. As Shakespeare says, 'All the world's a stage, and all the men and women merely players.'

Some people believe that our Third Eye is not only the window to our Soul but acts as a camera recording the inner and outer depths of our lives to be played back to us in the After Life. The brow chakra represents the self-realisation stage in adults when we realise that we are not defined by our past or negative experiences but that we are simply spiritual beings in a human body having a human experience that enables our Souls to expand, develop and grow. We realise that we are simply extensions of each other and our goal is to live in harmony with ourselves and others. As we are human, this state of being is incredibly difficult to maintain on our journey through Earth, however this realisation lies deep within us all.

The Sanskrit word *Ajna* means 'to perceive' or 'command' and is linked to our perception and memory. When our brow chakra is blocked, we may lack the ability to see or perceive things clearly; we may be disillusioned or lost. We may suffer from a poor memory or seem detached or removed from reality.

A clear chakra enables us to see things as they really are; understand exactly who WE Really Are. We are able to sustain focus, have a laser sharp memory and exude creativity and imagination. A clear brow chakra enables us to have a clear vision of our goals, pathway and intuition.

If our brow chakra is overactive we may become delusional,

experience and create circumstances in our mind that are not really happening. It is imperative that chakras remain balanced. We must remember that although we are spiritual beings, we are living a human existence and so we must remain grounded.

Indigo

Indigo is a very spiritual colour. It symbolises spiritual wisdom and self-realisation. It is linked with intuition and heightens our levels of concentration. Indigo represents service to humanity, sincerity and integrity. Indigo is associated with devotion and religion, namely Christianity, and used in religious clothing. It is a deeply rich colour, a perfect mix between midnight blue and violet, and connotes status and wealth. In fact, during the Elizabethan era, only those of a high social standing were allowed to wear indigo. Because indigo dye was rare and expensive, sumptuary laws were created that permitted only the privileged to wear this color.

Whilst blue is the colour of communication, indigo is the colour of personal thought and inward thinking thus making this a very inspirational colour. Indigo is a great colour for inventors to use for 'out of the blue' thinking! Research proves that indigo stimulates the right brain or creative activity and helps with spatial skills. A perfect colour for dancing!

Negative effects of indigo are linked to fanaticism and addiction.

'*The Indigo Children*[7] *lead with a machete, cutting down anything that lacks integrity.*'-Doreen Virtue[8]

[7] Find out more by reading *The Care and Feeding of Indigo Children by Doreen Virtue.*

STRONG WOMAN

Strong Woman
When you feel neglected
Cherish Your Self
Know that You are the Author of Your own journey
And Evolve Your Self

Strong Woman
When you feel rejected
Accept Your Self
Know rejection is a state of mind
And Evolve Your Self

Strong Woman
When you feel used
Appreciate Your Self
Know that nobody defines You
Know that You are loved more than you can ever know
And Evolve Your Self

Strong Woman
When you feel abused
Love Your Self
For nobody can Love You better
Trust Your Self
Heal Your Self

Strong Woman
When you feel ignored
Recognise Your Self
For You have always been here
Before, during and thereafter
Know Your Self

Strong Woman
You are made of strong stuff
Survived hardships and struggles and still came out tough
Always keep that little bit of Love
For Your Self

Strong Woman
You are always giving
But be wary Goddess, you are not living for others
For you have Your own plight
Keep within You a balance of strong mettle and an
abundance of Love and Light

Being a Strong Woman does not mean being aggressive
It's possessing the Knowledge and Power to know what you
deserve
And the wisdom to know better
Be an Inspiration, a Pioneer, an admired Trendsetter

Take control of Your journey for it is Yours and Yours alone
Take heed of others' dramas- they are just that
Do not allow others to define You, validate You, use You,
abuse You
Think ever positively about Yourself
Honour Your journey for this Life will soon be over
Too late to start over

Acknowledge Now
Cherish. Accept. Appreciate. Love. Recognise
The Beauty of Who You Really Are
For You are truly wonderful
Heal and evolve because you sincerely are A Star

Daniella Blechner, 34, London, England

IN YOUR EYES ...

When you look at me and smile,
I see your soul
It's abundant and located in a place further than walking miles would ever take me
The place is resplendent, sacred and laced with no lies but a river flowing with truth
The place is not selfish or plagued by haste but surrounded by serenity and the taste of eternity
For to us, forever is now—the visage of the two of us
Naked eyes can't see or decipher this
For only those dressed and ready to dive naked into your ocean like me
Have this power to look and see through your eyes...

Anyiko, 26, Molo, Rift Valley, Kenya

LIGHT

Light in my night
So that in my darkest hour I may shine as bright.
Force upon me vision in spite
So I may see deceit in hindsight.

Rays of light upon my steel
Steady my arm, strengthen my shield
Bury the slayed, force them to feed
On the mud beneath my feet

Burn my sins and purge me free
Sear the wounds, close them seal
So I may retain what remains of me
Split the chains twining their seeds

Then blanket me as I dance
Warm my spirit as I laugh
My smile is yours as I reach for your source
Embody a man so I may love him pure

Alesha Aris, 24 Kingston, Jamaica

MY LOVE FOR YOU

*dedicated to Bob Schubert

My love for you emits cerulean, azure -- all shades of blue.
It speaks in Sanskrit to all, 'tween us: an esoteric tongue only
we know.
My love ne'er veils, nor vails.
My love scoffs at shackles and chains and barbed wire
tipped walls.
My love is best mates with the sun and all of Milky Way
Galaxy's quasars.
My love surrounds with no bounds, ne'er smothers.
My love loves with a love of mother, lover, Gaia, god/dess.
All-encompassing: needs not compass to find its way for its
everywhere in every layer of existence.
My love is not only
mine, it's yours, ours.
Your love emits crimson.
Our love emits indigo.

Eva Xanthopoulos, 24, Cleveland, USA

FUTURE

I sit down and I paint a life
My imaginary twins and I paint a wife
With a heart like a dove she's the angel type
I thank God that he's blessed me with you in my life
She keeps annoying me and telling me I'm too nice
to the twins- that I spoil them, she's too right

She's the queen of the house and the kids know it
She demands all respect and the kids show it
Four boys one girl- she's the princess
Little diva and she knows when I've been stressed
I'm the king of the house but I hope you know
It's the women in the family that hold a home.

And I pray the devil doesn't
brush my paint away. It's my future and only God can pave the way
but one day I'll look back and I'll thank God that my paintings come true and the pain's gone

Francis, 26, London, England

LOVE'S VACATION

How am I going to say this without being cliché? I'm a sucker for a nice smile these days.
I pray these days- the girl that I'm praying for is prayerful
And she's not going to play me she prays that I never fall
Amen.
The sort of girl that gets love from my team mates, take her abroad and spend time in a heat wave

As for me I'm a natural guy. I'm always on a natural high so I had to find a natural wife
so I really gotta try put my all in
got me a girl that looks nice in the night and the morning.
You don't need the make up your brain makes up for it,
talking all day still waiting up for it.

I always told God that I didn't want to manage
Now I thank God that he's given me a queen and a palace.
Every time I see you it's like the first time, and I got an eye full I'm not talking about Paris

And now we embark on a journey,
We don't have to drive we can walk through the park in the early
And I can do the romance thing because a real man knows romance is a real man's thing.

Your friends might say I'm too good to be true but ask 'em is there anyone too good for
You?

Francis Sanni, 26, London, England

YOU ARE...PART 1

...my inspiration
The cornerstone of my focus
A part of my concentration
Undiluted, pure
Attaining a higher self
A mystical vibration

...my proclamation
A vocal veneer
A vibrant visualisation
Pronouncing, announcing
A uniqueness of strength
Steeped in years of determination
An eternal continuation

...my exclamation
Heart skips a beat,
A mouth-watering manifestation
A yearning, wanting, longing
Loins burning, stomach churning
Make love until early morning
A new type of dawning

...mesmerising
Tantalising, satisfying, gratifying
Every cell in my body
I'm not lying
Straining, staining, holding
My being in a grip
Factualising, justifying, simplifying
How to be
How not to slip

...captivating
Joining, uniting, aligning
Grasping my soul
Enhancing my meditation
Flowing through my veins
A sensuous, sweet, sensation

...my compulsion
Pushing, pulling
Trying, guiding
Taking, leading
Believing yet feeling
Visioning, dreaming
Promoting, seeing
Our potential
Our spiritual meaning

...my motivation
Challenging me to see
Enhancing all I'm destined to be
Walking beside
A satisfaction
A counteraction
A people's continuation

...my construction
Helping us to build
Our foundation
Captured from an Ancestral tradition
Blessed by Our Creators personal function
A positive capitalisation
A consistent, constant captivation

…my completion
Fulfilling a journey
Towards our destination
A walk
A trip
An excursion
Blessed
Taking us to our spiritual conclusion

Kwame McPherson, London, England

Positive Affirmations

I see that I am the creator of all that appears within my Life and I take control for the Life that I live.

I can see and think clearly

I can clearly see that problems exist within my Life and I am fully able to provide solutions to these problems

I have an Inner Guidance System and Intuition that always brings about positive outcomes in my Life

I am able to see, hear and listen to what my Intuition is telling me and know that this Intuition operates for my highest good

I am a Child of God and God speaks to me through my Intuition and Soul

I can see the Truth clearly and see all things and people for what and who they truly are.

I remove all negative blocks that are preventing me from seeing or acknowledging the Truth in all people, places and things today.

Crown Chakra
(Sahasrāra)

The crown chakra, also known as the Sahasrara in Sanskrit is located at the crown of the head, commonly known as the 'soft spot' on an infant. It is believed to be the bridge to the cosmos and higher worlds. It is seen as the door to a higher state of consciousness and awareness, and is seen as a direct link to universal energy. It takes one beyond the physical and material state of being and back to the true nature of our purpose and being.

It is believed that when we come to Earth we experience separation from God causing our crown chakra to close down. This creates a sense of aloneness and isolation; this separation from All That Is is human consciousness. The opening of this chakra causes a sense of acceptance and understanding that we are in fact one unified body perfectly connected to God but carrying our individual lives and experiences on Earth.

The crown chakra represents a period in our lives where we are self-realised. We no longer perceive things as 'wrong' or 'right', 'good' or 'bad' and accept these polarities as part of human consciousness and tapestry. We understand that life is a series of lessons designed to enable our Soul to grow and evolve. We understand that everything we experience is part of our purpose and that we are all inherently connected to each other through God's unconditional Love.

When the crown chakra is balanced we have access to universal energy and our subconscious mind. At this state, we are able to reach higher levels of consciousness and are more likely to reach our full potential.

When the crown chakra is blocked, our lives may lack meaning; we may feel a loss of identity or purpose and struggle to understand our place in the world. We may lack direction and focus and experience a sense of hopelessness.

When the crown chakra is overactive, we may become susceptible to 'far out' experiences and struggle to separate fantasy with reality. Some may even develop a sense of grandeur and delusion. Whilst keeping our chakras balanced is important, it is imperative that we remember that although we are spiritual beings living a human existence, we must remain grounded and centred at all times.

Violet

Violet is another colour that is linked with nobility and royalty. It is a rich colour that also connotes wealth. Conversely, violet is a very spiritual colour. It represents a sense of existing 'beyond the physical realm' and links to a higher state of consciousness. Violet is a humanitarian colour and is associated with wisdom, humility and service. Violet is a magical and mystical colour and promotes imagination and represents dreams.

Violet is the colour of judgement. Being a mixture of red and blue, it represents this sense of duality and polarities. Blue represents the cool and collected aspect whereas red represents the dynamic and fiery aspect. Violet syncs these two colours together in perfect harmony and is also therefore a fantastic colour to use for meditation. From a psychology standpoint, violet promotes harmony and peace of mind; it brings stability and peace.

In Western and Eastern cultures violet is associated with mourning rituals. In Christianity it is associated with Advent and Lent and in Iran violet signifies an omen for the future. Did you know Leonardo Da Vinci declared that meditation and prayer are ten times more powerful when praying under a violet ray of light, as can be found in church windows?

- ♥ **Mauve:** judgement, justice, good decision making, rational thought, higher aspirations.
- ♥ **Lavender:** fragility, vulnerability, sensitivity.

- ♥ **Lilac:** implies immaturity, superficiality and youthfulness.

'Forgiveness is the fragrance that the violet sheds on the heel that has crushed it.'

— *Mark Twain*[9]

[9] American author of '*The Adventures of Tom Sawyer*' and its sequel, *'Adventures of Huckleberry Finn'*, the latter often called '*The Great American Novel*.'

TRUE LOVE

What is the true meaning of the word 'Love'?
The thing is, 'Love' has so many meanings!
So when you say to me "I love you"
Do you mean you're in love with the way I *look*,
Or the way I make you *feel*?
Or you love the way I walk, talk, laugh, smell or appeal?

Is it my *smile* that captivates you?
Or the way I wear my *hair*?
Or is it the *clothes* I wear that makes you stop and stare?

Or is it that you love *me* because of how I treat *you*,
With **T**ender **L**oving **C**are?
I cook for you, I clean for you, I massage you
I dote on YOU.

Or do I love you for what you can give me
A nice home, fancy car, a lovely family
Security...

Do I love you with all sincerity?
Or am I just thinking of me?

What is the true meaning of the word 'Love'?

True Love is a commitment of the *heart*
Right from the start it says
"I choose to love you, whether we're together or apart"

Love never fails.

True Love says “I’m going to be **patient** with you,
When you try my patience, I’ll still love you”

Love never fails.

True Love is **kind**; it sows a seed
It’s **helpful, merciful and benevolent** to those in need
Love never fails.

True love **is never envious** of what I have,
But it inspires you to reach your own goals
And doesn’t boast when it does.

Love never fails.

True Love **isn’t proud** – pride comes before a fall!
But in Love you can stand tall.

Love never fails.

True Love **isn’t rude or selfish**
And doesn’t feel the need to be loud,
Or to always have centre stage in a crowd.

Love never fails.

True Love **isn’t easily angered**,
It forgives and forgets
Even when it’s difficult,
And it leaves no regrets.

Love never fails.

True Love **always protects**
And when I’m down in the dumps

Never rejoices in my downfalls,
Only in my triumphs.

Love never fails.

True Love **always trusts**, never accuses,
Always hopes, never doubts
Always perseveres, never gives up.

Love never fails.

I love you unreservedly
And can you say you love me, unconditionally?

LOVE NEVER FAILS.
(based on 1 Corinthians 13)
Cezanne Poetess, 40 something, London, England

SELF-OFFERING

Love often carries no defence,
Open and Giving,
I have often surrendered in love
My partner eclipsing all man and all woman.
They are my breath,
The fog that I exhale,
As I intoxicate myself in their aroma,
Gently I inhale.

Love is not complacent,
Its optimism at its peak,
It keeps us growing in each other,
As we embrace its currency.

Love is not worthless,
It's deluxe at its best,
But never be disillusioned by love,
For within love trials are set.

However love overrides all of life's demands
It keeps you growing in each other's arms,
It's the splendid passion at its brightest
It's a forever beautiful charm.

To those that defy love,
Reject it as they dwell in disillusioned flaws,
Demise to heart will become their energy
A deficit above them all.

Love is not miserable,
Although challenging it defines who we are,

An attitude of greatness,
Not disjointed only prosperous.

Translate me the one I love,
Show me the way,
Open my spirit to such a feeling,
In a loving way.
Show me your treasure
I sacrifice myself in your name,
I will not be disheartened by your promise
As I introduce your preface.
There is so much to you sweet love,
Far more than the four letter word,
So now I allow love in love to be my earth.

Love allow me to be your witness
As you become my premium account,
Posture yourself inside me
Let love not stray only breath take.

Darren Moxam, 35 London, England

AFTER THE RAIN

After the reign
even so sovereign
there comes a change
without exchange.

after my loneliness
after my suffering
I stumbled upon a princess
and here I am smiling

for sure it is said
That after the rain
comes the rainbow.

Mtu Fisi

UNCONDITIONALLY

don’t love with conditions
and parentheses and quotation marks
and doodled brackets around the reasons
why today you love him but tomorrow you are unsure

love him in every breath
in every syllable that you utter
love him in the way he sometimes
slurps his coffee and he always loses his page
in the book he is reading
love him in the way you are always cold
and his hands are always colder
love that he is not the completion of you
but the addition of your story

love him even when his voice gets soft and scared
even more so when he is unsure
when he is a little lost
a little sad
wondering if the path he is on is the right one
prove that you want to walk alongside him
even when you are inhaling dust and you cant
stop coughing and your eyes are
starting to burn

love him even when he eats all the leftovers
the ones you looked forward to all day
love him even as he talks to you over your favorite movie
or thought you were listening while you were studying
love him because

he loves you
without brackets and quotation marks

he loves you even when you aren't listening
even when you make fun of the way he loses his page
his path
his footing even when you are scared
and small and frozen
he has loved you

forget your withering soul
and drop the conditions
the barriers
just love

Kate Robinson, 20, State College, Pennsylvania

THE JOURNEY

Smooth, like a road freshly laid, no potholes or speed bumps, sunny skies; no clouds or rain

Pleasurable company, great tunes coming through, tank is on full, enjoying the view.

Starts slowly at first, road ahead not so clear, there's a slight incline up and a bend getting near

Put the brakes on the speed, things are starting to cool; there are clouds in the distance moisture starting to pool

First a flash then a crack, first the light then the sound, blue skies have all vanished, water soaking the ground.

Bumpy and jerky, unsteady to steer, the road signs mean nothing, all blurry unclear.

But...

Just as the way ahead looks dark and at its most unfriendly, and the steering wheel is gripped with anticipation as the fuel gauge hovers above empty...

A warm reassuring hand slides across the back of the driver's neck, the fingers are extensions of the passenger's forgotten love, loyalty and respect.

The driver turns, his eyes say, I don't know if we're going to reach where we're supposed to be…

The passenger's eyes look back and say wherever it is; we'll be together… just you and me.

Anonymous

DENOUNCING DEATH

It must have been tragic how we died.

Forced to wait for another time
The other must of suffered from the lurking lost
A lover dead, a lover gone
Cursing and begging their God to return to them and make death undone
Until they too crawled into the dust.
Transcending leaps against time to grow and breathe again, spirit wise
In a different paradigm
So that when they meet they will resume, recover and release the pause.

Strangers today with a century old love

Alesha Aris, 24, Kingston, Jamaica

REAL LOVE

real love is about respect,
not about keeping the other in check
love is inspiring the other to keep aspiring
keep evolving
together solving
real love doesn't exist in time, nor is it intricate
It's infinite
Simple and intimate

real love is about acceptance,
acceptance of all that was, is and will be,
love isn't wrapped up and frilly
real love hasn't got much time for ribbons and bows,
fancy lines and prose -it's not about material shows
love cannot decrease, it only grows

real love is unconditional
regardless
facadeless

Real love doesn't come with terms and conditions
With booby traps and secret missions
Love works best when each other listens
love needs space to move and flourish
love needs love for it to nourish
love isn't fearful or insecure
love isn't addictive -needing more and more
real love is unconditional, everlasting and true
love is for all, not for the few

real love is seeing my hair in the morning and not running a mile
at the worst of his jokes still raising a smile
encouraging them in the right direction - even if it means seeing less of them
real love doesn't judge, nor can it be measured
real love is permanent and should forever be treasured love
is respecting each other's individuality
real love isn't binding, love sets you free

real love doesn't diminish when they aren't 'who you want them to be'
-'programmed' them to be
real love is the Power of honesty
real love has no expectations, only the Truth we see
Truth of the other in all their shining Glory
The Good, the Bad, the Ugly
.....
Love is to Truth as Simple is to Be.

Danlella Blechner, 34, London, UK

LIVE OUT LOUD

And we would laugh so hard
to bust apart the madness,
that tears would wash away
the ailments that serious often brings.
Setting fire to the pile of rules
we make and break in everyday,
what a comical drama we build
In this shifting play of time,
slipping by, no reason or rhyme,
thoughts indulge in scrutiny
and try to hold onto to a 'what'
As 'when' and 'why' change every 'how'.
Find reason to harp about weather
and the wind will change its tune,
try seeking to understand this life
and the dust of dreams will pass you by.
Let crying only follow in laughter
Let stomping only follow in dance
Let shouting only call out in Love
stress only to emphasize kindness.
We are fire flies in twilight of time
spreading light from one to another
our glow dulls in the fading mundane
so laugh carefree and live brightly
before this good season sweeps us away.

Jeffrey Vionito, 39, Dallas, Texas, USA

Positive Affirmations

I am a Beautiful creation and representation of God. No one is below me, no one is above me.

I accept and understand that everyone is on their own individual journey and I choose to make a positive contribution.

I forgive myself for all of my mistakes. I am perfect in God's eyes.

I accept and understand that Life is a series of lessons and experiences that allow my Soul to evolve, grow and learn in its own time.

I awakened to my Life's purpose now and am ready to inspire and empower others through the fulfillment of my Dreams.

I choose to turn my negative experiences into opportunities and blessings for through them I grow stronger and wiser.

I accept and understand that I am connected to all people and all things and I have the power to affect them positively.

I accept and understand that I am part of a bigger plan and my place in the world is vital.

I do not judge others. Judgment is borne of fear and the only thing truly real in Life is Love.

I ensure that all of my actions, words and intentions are positive and for the Highest Good.

~Love Never Ends~

Quotes on Self Love, Life and Letting Go

By Daniella Blechner

'The Earth breathes. Just as we do. The Earth feels, just as we do. The Earth Loves, Provides, Forgives and Nurtures. Even in the midst of devastation and inflicted destruction- it comes back. Even in the midst of attack-it comes back. It comes back to Nurture us, to Love us. It keeps on breathing, keeps on evolving, changing and remoulding. We can learn a lot from the Earth.'

'Love can be so simple sometimes for it can be the tiniest things that can draw out the most Powerful Emotion.'

'Our appetite for Life and Love, even if suppressed for a time, will always instinctively return.'

'Through the darkness, we must believe in time the Light will Shine.'

'When we hear the whisperings of our instinctive gut feeling…Go with our intuition...Be silent and listen.'

'We can only trust another to be all that they are. With this is mind, in time, we can learn to Forgive.'

'Today I emancipate myself from past hurts and pains and make a pledge to Fly the Future a Lighter Soul.'

'A wound takes time to heal,

A plant takes time to grow,

Healing takes time to manifest

Seeds take time to sow

Let Life unfold and in time it will

blossom.'

Maslow's Law

Abraham Maslow was a Brooklyn based psychologist who developed the Hierarchy of Needs model and published his paper 'A Theory of Human Motivation' in 1943. He was primarily interested in what motivates people. In his paper he explains his theory that people are motivated by a set of needs. These needs were set out in a tier system in the style of a pyramid. When each set of needs was fulfilled, it was the natural order that we seek to fulfil the next.

Maslow's Law explained.

- Our first set of needs is **basic and physiological.** These needs are things we depend upon for survival. For example, eating, drinking, shelter and generally healthy bodily functions. Sexual needs are also classified as basic and physiological. We need to reproduce for the survival humankind.
- **Safety.** Following on from our basic and physiological needs, we need to feel a sense of safety that our needs will be met. We begin to seek security in people we are around and the environment that surrounds us.
- **Love and belonging** are needs that become apparent as we progress further up the chain. Once we feel secure, we begin to crave a sense of belonging and acceptance whether through friendships, intimate relationships, family, social settings, or work.
- **Esteem.** When our basic, security and social needs are met we turn to look within. We begin to seek a sense of independence and achievement. This creates a feeling

of self-esteem and self-worth through mastery and achievement of some sort. We may seek recognition and approval from others.

- **Self-Actualisation.** This is similar to what Carl Jung refers to as individuation.[10] It is about the desire to explore more of our potential and seek a sense of personal growth and purpose. Those at this level seek to experience out of the ordinary 'peak' experiences; experiences that would alter their lives dramatically. It was with this in mind that Maslow added a sixth concept called **Self-Transcendence.**
- **Self-Transcendence** depicts the desire to go beyond the human level of consciousness and experience unity and a higher truth. This higher truth links to understanding who we are in the greater sense of the world and feeling a part of a greater whole: a 'oneness.'

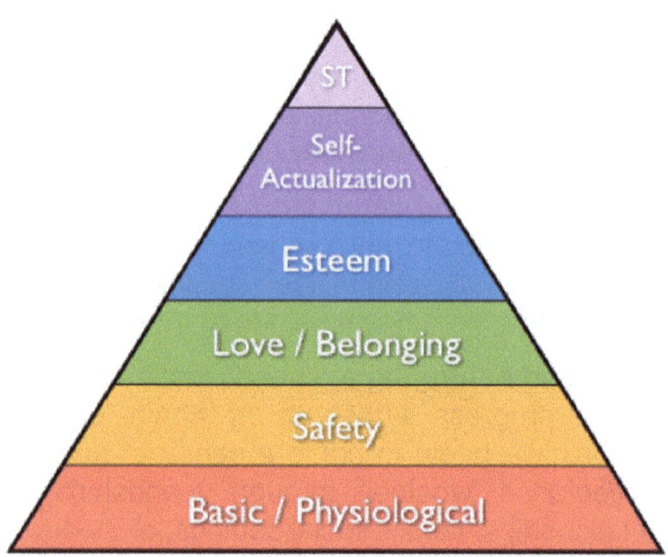

[10] describes the manner in which a thing is identified as distinguished from other things.

BIOGRAPHIES

I am honoured to be able to present these talented poets involved in the compilation of '7 Shades of Love'. These individuals are all beautifully unique and inspiring. They are an eclectic mix of different ages, races, cultures and religions who have come together from all across the world to share their message on a universal theme: Love. Please read their bibliographies and find out what inspires them.

ATHZIRI COCILION

Athziri Cocilion, 21, is currently a student majoring in Biology. She was born September 19th, 1992 and has lived in rural Illinois her entire life. Between the ages of twelve and fourteen Athziri found adjusting to adolescence difficult. In order for her to deal with those 'growing pains' she resorted to writing as an outlet to cope. Writing is the prefect escape for Athziri. It's a way to express her inner feelings, and poetry is a life-long love of hers.

More recently, it has become the best way for her to let out her sadness and frustrations about her failed relationships and bad taste in men. 'The Fear Inside' is a piece written while she was still casually seeing her current boyfriend. Having previously been in a very toxic, destructive relationship, she writes about being afraid of repeating that negative experience. 'The Fear Inside' is an autiobiographical piece about a woman who wants to give her partner everything but is unable to so due to a fear of getting hurt or being used; this always holds her back.

'Risky Business' is about that same man and how she finally decides that she could not let the past cloud her judgment in this completely different situation. The woman in the poem comes to the realisation that they are two different men and that if she ever wanted to be happy again, she had to trust that he was going to be different If it meant it was going to be short-lived, at least she could breathe knowing she had given her all.

You can see more of her work at http://acocilion.wordpress.com

SIMONE DUNBAR

Simone Dunbar's love affair with the written word started as an avid teenage reader whose love of the work of Caribbean and other authors inspired her to write short stories. Simone, who hails from Ocho Rios, St. Ann - Jamaica's garden parish, has had several poems published in the Arts & Literature section of *The Sunday Gleaner* under the pseudonym DSD. Her poem 'Dale's Parents' was previously selected as poem of the week. Simone found her niche in poetry when she started writing poems as a means of, in her words, 'speaking my boyfriend's language' since he is also a writer and their relationship was the inspiration behind her two most recent pieces.

JEFFREY VIONITO

Jeffrey Vionito is the author of, *The Heart That Never Breaks.* The poetry in this book is a reflection of his spiritual journey since 2010, when events took place in his life that brought him to a realization. This realization was a shifting point of clarity that he had discovered through means of meditation and other spiritual practices. Since then, he has been writing as a way to maintain awareness and deepen his understanding of the many teachings that the inner journey has to offer.

The two poems found in this book, 'Refuge of Love' and 'Live out Loud' are inspired by a constant journey of spiritual awakening.

'So often we lose awareness of the many experiences we should be in immense gratitude for. The conditioning of a busy life with busy thoughts can sometimes bear an illusion of drama and incompleteness. It is only when we begin to look within, and learn to live from a quieter place of being, that we realise the abundance that surrounds us. As I cultivated this philosophy, I began to experience the subtle scent of the divine work its way through my life. And in this experience I found an even deeper love for my wife, family, and felt a natural joy breathe a sigh of levity into my everyday living.'- Jeffrey Vionito

Jeffrey's work can also be viewed in publications such as 'The Elephant Journal' and on his website at

www.freedomoftheheart.com.

E. LEE CALECA

Lee Caleca is a freelance writer and New Jersey native who began fine art training at age 11. She's worked in many mediums including pastel, oil, watercolor, acrylic painting, clay, plaster of Paris, textiles, wood, and natural fibers.

With early training in voice and jazz dance she's appeared in newsprint, theater, on camera, on stage and runway, and has held responsibilities including professional photography, location assistant, set design, property, casting, and costume design and execution.

She's currently a judge for the Global Ebook Awards and the Eric Hoffer Small Press Awards. She holds a Bachelor of Applied Science in Fashion Design, is a 2x Juice Award winner for Fresh Design & Outstanding Use of Creative Perspective by the International Academy of Design and Technology, and has received the HubNuggets Award for Best New Writer by HubPages.

'The inspiration for 'Now I Am Grass' came from a love affair with a world traveler, someone with home I could never seem to connect on a deeper level. 'Riverpool' was the result of loving too much and falling too fast.'

'For me, creative writing always begins as a spontaneous moment. Between inspiration and the final product, there is always frustration, desolation, and accountability for the words I arrange on a page to make felt what cannot be seen. In the end though, we secure each other through the connection of our emotions. We are the storytellers and the dreamers of dreams who do our best to bring glory to the age of man.'

Where to find E. Lee Caleca online:

http://calecaworld.blogspot.com/
https://www.smashwords.com/books/view/118849
http://www.amazon.com/Creekwood-E-Lee-Caleca-ebook/dp/B008536VF2
http://couturepopcafe.blogspot.com/

DARREN MOXAM

Darren Wayne Moxam was born in 1978 in North West London. He spent his childhood in the vibrancy of the city. It was an influential witness to his growth through his first steps into school to his final steps at university.

As a young man, literature played a role of significance but remained peripheral to his fascination of female black role models. A level of admiration resided in such role models as Oprah Winfrey, Iyanla Vanzant and Maya Angelou. Their views and interpretation shaped his own and in turn took him on a reading journey through poetry and spiritual awareness. Aged 20, he met a wonderful woman that he loved and cared for dearly; she went on to be the mother of his beautiful child but young love was premature of life experience and in those few years the terms of endearment retracted and came to an end. Relationships, Love, Devotion; Darren came to realise these words had their own contents pages. Literature came into the forefront of his focus. A medium of communication that projected expression became his outlet. It was a gateway for his enthralling words of love and pain and so his poetry soothed his turbulent emotions. 'Sometimes it takes obstacles or something traumatic to bring the thing most hidden in us to come to life.' he says.

Darren Moxam decided to broaden his writing style and challenged the idea of writing erotic short stories. His first story, 'Online Seduction', was showcased online and astonishingly received a great deal of attention. Darren's writing was a witness of progression and evolution of his writing style. Before long he wrote 'Sandra's Revenge' and released segments of the story in stages.

Darren progresses on his journey and is thankful to his audience, friends and family for their invaluable support. He believes that his ability to write comes from Jesus the most high and in the end it'll be by God's grace as to how far he goes.

www.darrenmoxam.com

WAKONYO GACHANJA

Wakonyo Gachanja (Waksy) 21, is a young aspiring poet born in Nairobi, Kenya. She began writing poetry when she was 13 years old, as an outlet of her negative emotions but it wasn't until she was 16 that she began sharing her poems with her friends. By then, poetry had become less of a chore and more of a passion. Her themes are mostly love-based.

Apart from writing poetry, Waksy is an upcoming musician (both a songwriter and a vocalist) and she hopes to someday dazzle crowds with her unique music. She is also studying Art and Design in the University of Nairobi.

During her free time Waksy enjoys reading novels, spending time with friends and family and watching movies (when she's not playing her gig). Some of her favourite poets include Pablo Neruda, and Warsan Shire, not to mention Rumi.

EVA XANTHOPOULOS

Eva Xanthopoulos, 24, is a Greco-American poetess, inspirational speaker, Shamanic Reiki Master, and multimedia artist from Cleveland, Ohio. She received her Bachelor's Degree in Creative Writing from Cleveland State University and has been writing poetry for a decade. Many of her works are published both in print and online. (*The Golden Lantern, Mystic Living Today, The Journey Magazine,* etc.) She's the author of the books *Water Walker* and Sacred Shapes. Additionally, she has published and edited a variety of poetry anthologies including *The Universe Inside, Confessions Beneath The Oak Tree,* and *Queen Me*. Eva is the founder of *Poehemian Press & Podcast, The Artistic Muse, BeLove BeLieve*, and is the co-founder of *Etheric Archives.*

For details about Eva's poetry and artistry visit:

www.theartisticmuse.com
www.evapoetex.wordpress.com
www.facebook.com/EvaPoetexArtist

NATALIE BRINHAM

Natalie Brinham works in Human Rights and International Development. She is also a humanist and proud mother of a five year old girl. She has spent the past decade living between the UK and Southeast Asia and currently lives in Malaysia. She wrote the poem five years into a marriage that was destructive and damaging, but loving at the same time. The main casualty of the relationship was her own identity and sense of self-worth. The poem reflects her experience of sudden and almost violent loss. In this poem, she uses memories of her marriage vows to reflect on how both love and social expectation can trap us and diminish our power.

She says,'Writing the poem helped me to begin to mourn for my sense of self. I wrote this poem five years into a marriage that has been destructive and damaging, but loving at the same time. The main casualty of the relationship has been my own identity and sense of self-worth - and my experience was one of sudden and almost violent loss . In this poem, I used memories of my marriage vows to reflect on how both love and social expectation can trap us and diminish our power. Writing the poem helped me to begin to mourn for my sense of self. As my marriage once again careers off on another destructive pathway, I am still searching for my power reserves. I know that one day I will again be able to hold my little self up for all to see.'

NICOLE MOORE

Nicole Moore is an experienced Creative Writing Tutor, Freelance Writer/Editor, Arts Consultant and Published Poet. She has taught creative writing as a writer in residence in Islington primary schools, at the Centerprise Black Literature Development Agency and as an Associate Lecturer for Open University. Her arts/literary projects have involved travelling to the US and the Caribbean, and include participating as a panel member at a Why We Write? conference organised by the Graduate History Association at Columbia University in New York. Her poetry writing is diverse and includes themes that explore issues of identity, gender, race, culture, and heritage.

Published Works:

Poetry:

June 2010 *No Time* in Sixty Poems for Haiti, a specially commissioned anthology, Cane Arrow Press

Published in *Poetry Today* Anthologies:

Dec 2000 ***Energy*** in Dreams and Desires
Oct 2000 ***High Spirits*** in The Passage of Life
May 1997 ***Silent Moments*** in Life Lines
Jan 1997 ***Colourless Entity*** in Word of Mouth

Edited Publications:

Aug 2010 ***Hair Power – Skin Revolution**** Anthology, Matador
May 2007 ***Sexual Attraction Revealed*** Anthology, AuthorHouse
Sept 2005 ***Brown Eyes**** *Anthology,* Matador
(*funded by The Arts Council England)

www.shawana-lulu.blogspot.com
www.shangwe2011.blogspot.com

EMMANUEL KARIUKI

Emmanuel John Kariuki, 24, lives in Nairobi, Kenya. He has a passion for writing poetry that people can relate to. His poems mostly reflect on real life issues and most of them are real life stories.

He is the proud father of a very handsome boy called Jabali which means 'The rock of Africa'.

He started writing poetry as a result of heartbreak. He did not even know he had such a gift until he begun to write about his pain.

Some of his hobbies include watching and playing football, writing poetry and socialising. One word of advice he would like to give people about love is to be careful who they fall in love with... Sometimes people are not who they really seem to be.

You can find Emmanuel's poems on his Facebook page below.

https://www.facebook.com/emmanueljj.kariuki

AMANDA EPE

Amanda Epe's previous published poetry and memoir writing has predominately waxed and waned on ethnic identity, culture and gender concerns and it is her first time musing on the power of love.

'It was an exciting and novel experience to contribute to the '7 Shades of Love' Anthology and also share my story in the 'Mr Wrong' book as it has enabled me to analyse and reveal my innermost thoughts.'

Amanda runs a project working on self-love/esteem and sexual health for girls and women so when she was asked if she would like to contribute it was so timely and she was enthusiastic at the prospect of contributing. Her story shared in Daniella's debut book, 'Mr Wrong', was a self-help tool for her and will possibly encourage other women who may have similar experiences in their relationships. Amanda's poetry on self-love was important to write because she is continuously working on self-acceptance and unconditional love as her basis, transforming her inner critic to self-praise and forgiveness. From her past experiences of unconditionally serving her 'King' and 'dethroning' herself i.e. my story in 'Mr Wrong' the 'How Do I Love Thee' Haikus were written to reinforce herself with the knowledge that successful relationships are built on self-love.

Amanda's debut book, 'A Fly Girl' travel memoirs on race, rage and relationships, will be available soon.

If you would like to read Amanda's blogs on self-esteem and sexual health visit www.msroseblossom.org

NICHOLAS BABBOU

Babbou Nicolas, 21, was born in a town called Kisii in Kisii County, Kenya. After completing his schooling in Kissii, he went on to become a student of Maths and Physics at Pwani University in Kilifi county at the coast of Kenya.

Nicolas is a humble guy who wants to fulfil his purpose in life.

He is inspired by what happens in his society and enjoys writing short stories and poems. The particular poem, *Jilted*, is about the pain he felt following a break up with a girl he loved very much.

LAWRENCE COKE

'"Love's Language" is a film idea that I had about a music producer who is totally in love with the process of music production as well as most forms of music. The universality of good music has fed into a strongly held belief for him that music must be the language of the soul as it does not matter where you are from or what language you speak, good music in all its forms will always stir something inside of you.

He finds himself falling in love with the cousin of his best friend, a writer who is visiting from overseas. She is completely in love with the written word as a form of expression, completely committed to the art and culture of the written word versus the spoken word. Her belief comes from the notion that when you talk, your words dissipate into thin air with only those within earshot able to hear; when you commit words to paper, you are giving birth to ideas potentially for ever...

Her point of view is somewhat influenced by the fact that she is deaf...

How does someone so in love with sound and music successfully express that love with someone who has never experienced it and has no desire to?

The first poem is her using the thing she loves (the written word) to explain why words, things that are spoken, are meaningless when weighed up against a person's actions.

His poem is a response to hers, but most of all a declaration of his love for her in her preferred way of communication, while urging her to consider the nuances and beauty in sound for him as another way to appreciate his feelings for her...'

MERCY TEKO

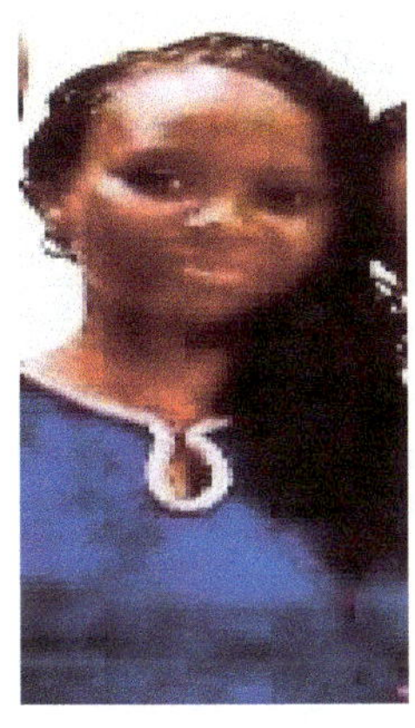

Mercy Teko is 18 and from Nairobi, Kenya. She studies Business and I.T in Strathmore University. Mercy always had a way of manipulating words to express exactly how she feels. Her inspiration for *The Blemished Resistance* was that she realised that love can help us overcome tribulations and insecurities. Her poetry ranges from Love poems to factual ones such as Tribalism, Religion and Drug Abuse. '7 Shades of Love.'

has given me an opportunity to finally let my light shine."- Mercy Teko

More of her work is featured in her friend's blog called *My Views Exactly*.

www.myviewsexactly.wordpress.com/2014/02/02/the-furnished-injustice/

GHADA KHORAYCH

Ghada Khoraych is a Toronto-based freelance writer. She holds a Master's degree in Sociology from the London School of Economics and Political Science and currently works in the health promotion field. Her love of writing grew from a young age, when she first learned to read and experienced the transformative power of fiction. Throughout her youth, writing was therapeutic and liberating, and her essays and short stories won acclaim in local writing contests.

Ghada self-published her first collection of poetry entitled *P oems by Ghada* in September, 2013. Written over a six-year period following her mother's death in 2003, this raw collection articulates the pain of loss and the need to make sense of it. Ghada's second collection of poems entitled, 'Inhale Exhale' was self-published in December 2013.

An avid blogger, Ghada has captivated audiences with her poetry and musings on life in her blog 'Unlearning the Fear.' Her blog was recently quoted in the February 2013 issue of Marie Claire magazine. Her writing explores themes of love, loss, society, mental health, and existential concerns. She's passionate about these issues, and volunteers her time to support marginalized populations.

This poem was motivated by a break-up, and the realization that, despite popular notions that 'love is all you need' sometimes, love just isn't enough. For the first time, I didn't wait until we hated each other. Instead, I acknowledged that we loved each other, but it wasn't enough to make it 'work'. For this reason, this poem symbolizes strength, courage and maturity.

Poems by Ghada
http://www.lulu.com/shop/ghada-khoraych/poems-by-ghada/hardcover/product-21277405.html

Inhale Exhale
http://www.amazon.com/Inhale-Exhale-A-Collection-Poems/dp/1494323648

Unlearning the Fear
http://unlearningthefear.wordpress.com/

DENIS MWANGI

Denis Mwangi, 20, studies Bsc Mechatronic Engineering at a local university in Kenya. Rapping is the main form of expression in his neighbourhood so he started out rapping with his friends. Soon after, he started writing poetry and now fuses his raps with his poetry to create spoken word.

He is a self-confessed, Mr. Wrong and admits to having broken a few girls' hearts. His poems are mainly about love and from a Mr. Wrong's perspective. He also writes about things that he grew up witnessing: difficult times he has gone through and sometimes he puts himself in someone's shoes and tries to express what they feel as creatively as he can. Denis loves describing, moments, feelings, scenes and emotions.

Check out his blog at: www.wordjusticeblog.wordpress.com

NJERI MU MUHIA

Winnie Njeri Muhia, 24 lives in Nairobi, Kenya. She is currently doing her diploma in Pharmacy at a college in Nairobi. She started writing poetry when she was about 18. It was a talent she stumbled upon. Since then, writing has been her hobby and she writes mostly about people and issues that surround us; like love and friendship. She writes to express her feelings, to affirm her faith and to release stresses that life can sometimes bring.

Winnie's blog: http://diaryofthepoet.wordpress.com/

DIANA GRAY LEWIS

Founder and CEO, The GenieInUs Foundation

Diana Gray Lewis or The GenieInUs Foundation, given to her in a vision to set up a 'motivational company', became a name known to many from her daily uplifting quotes and motivational messages that touched the heart of her readers. Using the famous social networking sites Facebook and Twitter is where it began back in 2008—her very 1st post read: *'Some people think it's holding on that makes one strong; sometimes it's letting go'.*

From there she picked up her passion and it became the motivation behind her thirst to reach out and uplift those who looked forward to her morning messages. A year later she was given the opportunity to spread the word on air, by becoming the first Lady to host a show for a local community online radio station, dubbing her slot as 'The Reposition Yourself Show', taking it to another level to reach out to those with her discussions on matters close to the heart, her fan based stretched as far as Japan. This poem was inspired by a friend and she actually wrote it the day before she was asked to perform at her very first spoken word event, unbeknown to her being the opening of a The Brent Civic Centre. This poem was also aired internationally on a New York radio station.

To find out more about GenieInUs Foundation check www.genieinusfoundation.com

ANYIKO OWOKO

Anyiko is a media personality, well known for her passion in arts and culture. She has previously worked for the BBC's International NGO – BBC World Service Trust's youth program Kimasomaso. She's also a TV Host and Assistant Producer of *Grapevine* on KBC, Kenya's longest-running Arts & Culture / Entertainment magazine show. Her high profile interviewees include Philip Bradley Bell, co- creator and lead writer of *The Bold & Beautiful* (*Guinness Book of World Records* longest-running TV soap series), international music stars Fally Ipupa, Akon and R&B legends Joe Thomas, Anthony Hamilton and Donell Jones, among myriad local stars and top directors of art institutions and projects.

Anyiko is a passionate writer and former Associate Editor of *UP Magazine*, Nairobi's leading arts and culture magazine. She's an established blogger on poetry, music and book reviews. In 2014, her blog, Black Roses, was named among Kenya's Top 25 Blogs to Follow by the Kenyan stem of the international destination website brand, *Travel Start*.

Anyiko is now a freelance writer with *Goethe-Institut Kenya* and *ARISE,* an international magazine on African fashion and achievements, among other notable local and international publications. Anyiko also curates art exhibitions. So far she has curated two: *Pure Art* by Eric Salisbury, American painter and muralist (2012 at Paa Ya Paa Arts Centre), and *Pieces of Fortune* by painter Edward Manyonge (2013 at Michael Joseph Centre). Anyiko is also the Sauti Sol Band publicist and has recently started Anyiko PR, a new company for Artist Image Consultancy and Events Curation.

Check out Anyiko's blog at www.anyiko.wordpress.com

ALESHA ARIS

While some chose music or visual arts, **Alesha Aris** took the path that allowed her to weave words into lyrical artistry.

Born in Kingston, Jamaica, her work slowly transitioned from private writing to an unearthing of a hobby up to a point of publicly showcasing tailored pieces. It was upon leaving the University of the West Indies that she sought to become more public with her work so that she may intrigue her audience by the virtue of rhythm, rhyme and imagery. Her inspiration ranges from casual observation to twining words to the rhythm of music.

When she's not writing you may find her developing and executing marketing tactics and being a volunteer aid within her community.

http://exoduspoetryjamaica.com/2014/01/21/alesha-aris-poet/

FRANCIS SANNI

Francis Sanni is a musician, poet and teacher. All aspects of his life and his vocation are underpinned by relationship with God The Most High.

He sees his art as an expression of an ongoing courtship with God which is expressed in an array of ways and these named above are just a few selected from a lifestyle of expression; a way of life.

He says, 'These poems chosen are a reflection of love. I feel the word 'love' has been misconstrued for some generations now. To me, love is an exertion, it isn't a feeling or a moment but a decision one makes to esteem one more that oneself. It's only the true embracing of love that brings forth fruits like true joy and its only God that brings such a commission and euphoria in fulfilling it.'

KWAME MA MCPHERSON

Award-winning author of short stories and poems, Kwame MA McPherson is a prolific writer and poet. Of Jamaican descent, Kwame's writing reflects his experiences and life observations. Significantly, as a Poetic Soul winner and author of short story books 'Deep Roots, Strong Tree' and J'amaica Vibrations', Kwame also has poetry works: 'Our Eternal Legacy' and T'o Our Fallen'. His first novel, 'The Paradise Embers' will be out in the New Year under the pseudonym, Anthony Angus.

He's a contributor to the phenomenal work Unbreakable by his friend, William Frederick Cooper's (U.S. launch date March 2014), and has provided his works to various anthologies including 'The Lime Jewel', a fund raising compilation for victims of the 2010 Haitian Earthquake.

Kwame likes enabling others to share and enjoy his Caribbean and life experiences through his eyes. He also aims to have his current and future works appreciated by an audience provoking thought, creating laughter and even causing tears by focusing on niche markets around the globe. But, in essence, he seeks to help others feel and encounter the world in all its glory.

Kwame's works can be viewed and purchased at:
www.lulu.com/spotlight/maxkey
and he can be contacted at:
www.kwamemcpherson.com

CEZANNE POETESS

Cezanne Poetess is a self-taught Visual & Spoken Word Artist and self-published author, guided by her in-tuition. Her work is a creative expression of her spiritual journey. She has been writing and recording her poetry since 2001, with 'True Love' being one of the first inspirational poems that reflected her Christian faith;

Cezanne believes that the feeling of Love is the highest frequency on which one can operate. She was inspired to write the poem 'True Love' to explore the different types of love, based on 1 Corinthians 13 in the Bible. She believes true love is unconditional, not based upon what you can *get*, but what you can *give*.

Cezanne currently resides in London, England; she is a happily single 40-something mother of three sons.

For details about Cezanne's poetry, art and self-help books visit www.cezannepoetess.com

KATE ROBINSON

Kate Robinson is a student at The Pennsylvania State University, studying English and Comparative Literature. She is endlessly searching for words and coming up with only more questions; this is mostly how her poetry is born. She writes mostly because it is the only thing that consistently makes sense to do.

My poem, 'Unconditionally', is more a whisper in the dark than anything else. It is an unrealized love more than an actual reality. It is a compilation of those who I have loved, it is a perhaps a dream or a prayer. At the end of it all it is probably nothing.'

http://whatwehavisthis.wordpress.com/

~Special Dedications to~

Francesca Blechner, Ron Blechner, Yvonne Blechner, Anthony Blechner, Renee Hirsch, Katie Blechner, Olivia Blechner, Naomi Kotler, Sue Patterso Reg Patterson, Gareth Duffield, Vicky Crumley, Lawrence Coke, Natasha Cameron and Steve Botham, Nancy Wheeler, Anj, Sophia Bailey, Rachael Tirstatine, Amanda Epe, Mavreen Brown, Cezanne Poetess, Kauljinder Joh Amde Anbessa-Ebanks, Shawn Peneloza, Charlie Innes, Leanne Moss, Jacq Weekes, Chris Warbarton, Matt Matthews, Daniel Fajemison-Duncan, Matthew Kinghan, Lauren Kirkman, Lola Atkins, Andre Farquharson, Lau Lartey, Ian Robert Sampson, Devron Callender, Segun Lee-French, Taru Khanna, Sarah King, Leah Noel, Cayman Grant, Seeds of Elevation, Ann Boswell, Adam Buck, Francesca Pritlove, DCosmic (Beyonder) and Marlor Palmer

~For your kind support and faith in my project. ~

www.ingramcontent.com/pod-product-compliance
Ingram Content Group UK Ltd.
Pitfield, Milton Keynes, MK11 3LW, UK
UKHW021830270726
14058UKWH00001B/68